DONOVAN:

New Beginnings

CR Wice

Dedication

For Dad

You always support me, without reserve

You believe in and encourage my creativity

Inspiring me to pursue my dreams

Making them come true

I love you

CHAPTER ONE

An unusual tension filled the room as the meeting ended on a Thursday morning in Las Vegas. Rodney and Donald were both curious about Marcus Donovan's distant demeanor. He appeared preoccupied, offering minimal feedback and seeming disengaged throughout the entire meeting.

"So, Marcus, does this wrap everything up, or is there something else you would like to address?" one of the men asked.

"Yes. I want to discuss your recent suggestion to add an employee to my team. I am still hesitant. But after much thought, having a personal assistant could be beneficial. That said, I want someone who has also trained as a security agent. I already have an impressive team. Putting someone else in the mix worries me—they need to be able to take care of themselves and me if necessary. I would like you to schedule a blind interview for tomorrow morning at my event center. Invitation only, of course."

Rodney, his managing agent, and Donald, his financial agent, have been employed for years. Both are surprised at his sudden acceptance. Several weeks earlier, they suggested he consider hiring a personal assistant, yet Marcus wasn't sure. He neither wanted a new employee nor felt the need to add to his current team. He never agreed or disagreed but promised to give it much thought and consider how it would affect his life. After reflecting on their reasoning, he realized that having an assistant could, in fact, be helpful.

Pleased with his acceptance, Rodney and Donald were still taken aback by the suddenness of his decision. Marcus noticed their exchanged looks and read their expressions.

"I know this is sudden. I never doubted your reasons for needing this position. To be honest, it was simple—I didn't want one. You both know how hard it is for me to let someone new into my circle and my life. But I took the time to think it over and realized you are right; this is what is best for me. Please find me the perfect assistant."

After hearing his verbal commitment, they began brainstorming how to assemble the interviews, one of which Marcus wanted scheduled for tomorrow. They asked if he had any specific guidelines or expectations. Marcus responded,

"Only one. It is best to wrap it up in a single day."

"We agree. It makes for a long day, but if done correctly, it works best."

They each had different reasons for preferring a quick, one-day event. Rodney and Donald worried that Marcus might change his mind if the process dragged on. Marcus himself remained anxious about the hire despite his agreement. He felt the quicker they completed the process, the better—"rip the band-aid off," as he put it.

"I plan to be there for the entirety," he continued. "This person needs to have qualities I can both live and work with. I need to observe their behaviors and have a say in who we choose. We are a team, but I must emphasize that I have the final say."

Marcus realized his words may have made him sound like a tyrant. In truth, behind his tough facade, he was nervous. He was satisfied with his current team. Before Rodney and Donald's insistence, it had never crossed his mind to add a personal assistant. Having someone new around him every day would be a tremendous change, something he would need to adjust to. Neither Bobby nor Mancuso, his trusted bodyguards, were with him daily.

"I want ten applicants. More than ten will complicate things, making a one-day event almost impossible. Only ten—no more, no less—or it does not happen."

Over the years, Rodney learned not to question Marcus once his mind was set. He knew Marcus did not want to hear objections like "planning this event on such short notice is too soon" or "ten applicants may not be workable." Those phrases were off the table.

So, they chose to take the win. Rodney and Donald decided not to voice concerns about the tight timeline. They would figure it out; they always did. The next twenty-four hours would be stressful, but they remained hopeful for a flawless outcome. Marcus needed an assistant, and now he was requesting one trained in security.

The real reason Marcus insisted on short notice—the elephant in the room—was the press. He didn't need to say it; they all knew. His biggest concern was the media. History had taught them that whenever they arranged anything involving Marcus, the sooner it happened, the better the chance of keeping it concealed and avoiding chaos.

Rodney had seen firsthand how the media seemed to have ears everywhere when it came to Marcus. They had no boundaries, no respect for privacy, and stalked his every move. While some reporters had good intentions, others sought to tarnish his image. All of them were desperate to capture a headline-worthy moment. Recently, paparazzi photographed him getting a haircut and manicure. The invasive photos landed on a magazine cover. Who wants pictures of getting a haircut on display for the world?

Marcus tries to lead a quiet life. When he wasn't performing, he self-isolates, which only makes the paparazzi hungrier. He worked hard to meet many of their demands. He agreed to public appearances, tried to stay transparent, remained busy with TV guest spots, sold-out shows, and charitable causes. He gives as much as he could to his fans and the media. Yet, it was never enough.

He is Marcus Donovan—a worldwide rock star, one of the most famous names in the world.

Knowing time was of the essence, Rodney and Donald began sharing interview information through their confidential network of professional contacts. Before long, CVs begin arriving. They sighed with relief when their efforts yielded nine qualified, confirmed applicants. Still, they are worried—Marcus had insisted on ten.

Uncertain of his reaction, they print and gather the nine for him to review. Rodney handed Marcus the CVs. After a thorough read, Marcus concluded all the candidates were impressive and well-experienced.

"Good job guys, but unless I am mistaken, I see only nine. I am not trying to be difficult, but I stand firm in my request for ten applicants."

"We know Marcus. We did our best. These nine are all that came in. We still have a few hours left; I am sure the tenth will arrive soon."

Marcus recognized he might sound unreasonable, but the number ten carried a personal meaning for him. It wasn't superstition—just history. The number ten had always brought excellent results in his life.

"I appreciate your efforts; all nine CVs look promising, but the event will not proceed without ten applicants. I already voiced my opinion on this," he reiterated.

The silence in the room grew uncomfortable. Rodney and Donald exchanged anxious glances.

Mancuso, a well-respected member of Marcus's security team, cleared his throat. Both Rodney and Donald interpreted this interruption as a positive sign. Mancuso was rarely far from Marcus during his detail, sharing responsibility with another trusted agent, Bobby. Over the years, Marcus had developed a strong bond with both.

Normally, Mancuso refrained from weighing in on Marcus's business decisions. His role was protection, not commentary. But today, he saw an opportunity he could not pass up.

"Please pardon my intrusion Mr. Donovan. May I speak?"

"Of course Mancuso. I would appreciate hearing your thoughts on this situation. Am I being unreasonable?"

Mancuso chose not to answer the question directly. Instead, he explained, "Sir, I notice your disappointment in not securing ten candidates. I also see Rodney and Donald share that disappointment. This is clearly a tense situation for all."

He was right. Rodney felt he had failed Marcus by not meeting his one demand. He didn't like the disappointment it caused. Options were running thin, and now everyone looked to Mancuso.

Mancuso considered whether he was overstepping by speaking in front of the others. Usually, his conversations with Marcus were private. But he saw no better time to act. With all eyes on him, he took a chance and spoke with confidence.

"I have information on someone who can fill the tenth spot. They are the perfect candidate."

He pulled folded papers from his suit jacket and handed them to Marcus. It was a CV for B. White, along with a formal letter of recommendation written by him.

The unexpected gesture stunned the three men. Why would Mancuso carry a CV and recommendation letter? None of them anticipated this.

Beth White was one of the best agents Mancuso had ever worked with. He recently learned she was searching for new opportunities. After her husband's passing, she took a job protecting a young pop star. Mancuso suspected the role was beneath her abilities. With her skills and adventurous spirit, she deserved more.

He left it to the group to decide. The CV spoke for itself. It was a Van Gogh in their field, painting a vivid picture of White's qualifications.

As the three men read the documents, Mancuso noticed their tones shift with interest. When they turned back to him, their expressions mixed surprise with approval.

"Tony, this is an outstanding CV. Do you know this B. White? Is everything here factual? Nothing is… exaggerated?" Marcus began to ask, his words trailing off.

Mancuso was pleased—they were curious. He hid a small smile.

"It is real. Everything you see is accurate. It's a strong CV, isn't it?"

The men smiled again. They were intrigued.

Rodney, attempting to remain neutral, finally said, "Contact them and set it up immediately. It looks like we have our number ten gentlemen."

Mancuso felt instinctively that White had a solid chance at the position. The challenge now was convincing her to fly from North Carolina to Las Vegas on such short notice for an anonymous interview. With little information he could provide, he hoped she would trust him.

She was adventurous, but would she accept such a last-minute offer? His instincts told him yes. He sent her a text immediately, stating he would call tonight. He crossed his fingers, hoping she would answer.

CHAPTER TWO

Beth White has returned to her home in North Carolina. She has been on a three-month stint as a personal security guard. Now, she finds herself with no immediate plans and is currently unemployed. Her employer, Sammie, decided she wanted to take some personal time off. She announced that with this tour over, she was taking a hiatus. She would be returning to the studio to write material and record her next album.

Although today marks an unknown beginning to what comes next, Beth feels a sense of relief at being home. She reaches for the latest bestseller that she started reading on the plane this morning. Even more, she is eager to relax in her own hot bathtub. Between the book and the bath, she hopes to wash away the loneliness of her empty home.

Four months ago, Beth landed a gig protecting a rising pop artist, Sammie. The young artist is personable, but she is also fearless and loves the limelight, which kept Beth on her toes. While it hasn't been Beth's dream job, the traveling and long hours occupied her time. She was searching for anything to fill the emptiness she feels when alone at home.

Enjoying a much-appreciated bath worked its magic, and she felt relaxed to be home. Beth put on her pajamas and prepared to settle in for a calm evening, then her phone rang. Her initial thought was annoyance, wondering who would be calling at this hour. She considered ignoring it, but she was also curious about the caller's identity. With a quick glance at the clock, she realized it was only 7:00 P.M. not as late as she thought. The long day of travel must have skewed her sense of time; she had been awake and on the go since 5:00 A.M.

The ringing phone finally stopped. Thank goodness! She only wanted to relax. She sat down with the remote to the TV, and now it was ringing again.

"Damn! Stop ringing! I don't want to talk to anyone right now— hush."

She was yelling at the phone as the ringing persisted. The caller was relentless, calling for the third time. Her curiosity finally got the better of her. She checked the caller ID—nope, she didn't know the number. Yet, it wasn't coming in as a spam call. Even though it was not a number she knew, it seemed familiar. Aggravated, she decided to answer, vaguely trying to hide her irritation.

"Hello."

She heard just one word and immediately recognized the voice.

"White."

It was her former sergeant from her time in the Military Security Forces, Anthony Mancuso.

"Hey Sarge, how are you?"

Not known for small talk, he got straight to the point.

"Did you get my text today?"

Beth knew from her experience collaborating with him to limit her questions and keep her responses brief.

"No, I've been on a plane all day. I just returned home after being on tour with my client for the last three months. Actually, as soon as I turned it back on, it started ringing."

Mancuso bypassed her detailed answer, expecting only a yes or no response.

"White, I have the perfect job opportunity for you. The catch is you need to move fast."

Something in his tone piqued her interest.

"Tell me more Mancuso."

Mancuso explained that a prominent individual was holding an interview event in Las Vegas tomorrow. Beth's head spun with the information. Having just returned home after three months on tour and a full day of travel, she felt tired and was eager for some time alone.

"Mancuso, there's no way I can make it to Las Vegas by morning, even with the time difference."

Mancuso, knowing her determination and drive, believed in her potential. He had trained and worked closely with her, knowing she was one of the best in the field; she thrived on challenges. If she thought she couldn't complete a mission, she would prove herself wrong.

"Well…" he paused, choosing his words carefully.

"I took a chance and signed you up for the interview. I already booked you a flight. It is the red-eye, leaving at 10:30 P.M."

He didn't give her time to respond and continued after noticing she had not immediately declined.

"It was an opportunity I felt you couldn't miss. This is a big one, White. I had an on-the-spot moment and threw your name into the mix. I believe you are the ideal candidate for the job. When these opportunities arise, there are no second chances, and as I said before, this one is significant."

As she processed the situation, a surge of adrenaline rushed through her. She had countless questions, but her instincts were to operate two steps ahead. In her mind, she was crafting a timeline, planning how to pack to ensure she arrived in Las

Vegas on time. Her heart raced, and for a moment she thought it might explode. This was the type of challenge Beth thrived on, lived for. She was always up for an adventure, and this sounded like the start of an exciting journey, one that was perfectly insane and entirely her style.

"So, let me clarify.

One, someone important needs security?

Two, the interview was advertised today, and it's happening tomorrow morning?

And three, you already bought me a ticket on the red-eye to Las Vegas?

Did I hear all this correctly?"

"Yes."

His flat and straightforward response didn't surprise her.

"Your timing is interesting, Mancuso. As of today, my current client has me on hiatus. She is returning to the studio."

Her mind was whirling with questions, but she decided to ask the most important one.

"Can I ask who this important person is, the one who waits until the last minute to hold an interview? I mean, who does this?"

It wasn't her intention for her question to sound sarcastic; she was merely asking out of curiosity. However, she sensed the unintentional snarky undertone in her voice. She was sure Mancuso noticed it too. She was about to clarify her question, actually apologize, but Mancuso didn't seem to mind her tone or bluntness.

"Sorry Beth, but it's called a blind interview event. There will only be ten interviewees. The position is for a personal assistant, who is also trained in security."

Beth considered the limited information for a moment. She knew time was of the essence, but she had many thoughts—multiple questions were racing through her head. Now he couldn't even reveal who this top-secret interview was for.

She exhaled, letting her thoughts catch up with her words as she weighed the opportunity. She was intrigued.

"Mancuso, my dear friend. Why do you tempt me with such an unusual opportunity? You know how I am."

"If I am crazy enough to agree to this, how do I know where to go? How do I navigate once I get to Las Vegas?"

Mancuso chuckled, thinking to himself, she is still my adventurous girl. He did notice her slight agitation, which momentarily concerned him she would decline. He was relieved that his offer had spiked her interest.

"Beth, I was hoping this opportunity would interest you. As I mentioned, I have already booked you on the red-eye flight; your ticket is waiting for you. You will arrive in Vegas at 7 A.M. A driver will pick you up at 8:00 A.M. The driver will have all the instructions, and he will know exactly where to take you for the interview. After the event, the driver will take you to the hotel; I have already reserved a room in your name."

Mancuso kept talking without pause. He didn't want Beth to decline the offer before he could provide her with all the information.

"Beth, I need to stress again that this is a once-in-a-lifetime opportunity. You just told me your client has gone back to the studio, so I see the timing is perfect. I know you, and I know you don't want to sit idly at home. After two days of this 'relaxing' you claim you want to do, you will be searching for something to fill your downtime. This opportunity will be amazing for you. We both know adventure is in your blood. You are made for it!"

"Sir, oh my goodness! You always know how to tempt me with a challenge. Lordy, you're gonna make the southern come out in me."

She was laughing but was only half-joking.

"So, what do you say? Are you getting on that plane tonight?"

Beth paused and took a big sigh. She had listened intently to everything Mancuso said. He wasn't wrong. To say she lacked a spark of adventure and excitement would be an understatement. She chose her following words carefully.

"So, it sounds like you have really gone out on a limb for me. It appears as if the next move is mine. I need to get packed and head to the airport, fast."

Mancuso let out a sigh and was laughing when he realized Beth was saying yes. He felt like a kid on Christmas morning who had received the shiny red bike he had begged Santa for.

"White, trust me. I promise this will be a great adventure. These interviewing events are by invitation only, and the experience will be worth every minute. If by chance you do not blow them away with your talent, which is very unlikely, please plan to stay the entire week in Las Vegas on me. I will send you a detailed text with all the information we have discussed."

Her mind was jumbled with all the information. The excitement of taking a last-minute trip across the U.S. to attend an anonymous interview, with no information—yes, she must be crazy. Yet they both knew it was her kind of crazy. Memories flooded back to her active days in the military; she never knew when, where, or who she would provide security for, sometimes at the last minute.

She thanked Mancuso for considering her for this opportunity. He assured her he would see her while she was in Las Vegas, possibly after the interview event.

She hung up the phone and rushed from the room to grab her suitcase. She dumped the current contents onto the bed, giving as much thought as time allowed, choosing the appropriate clothing for this last-minute trip. She packed both her luggage and a carry-on. She smiled as she wondered if she had packed too much. Nope, she justified her reasoning. She wasn't just packing for the interview; she was also preparing for a week-long stay in Las Vegas. She needed choices. However, she was still a bit concerned about all the last-minute secrecy, but who doesn't love a free trip to Vegas, right?

***

Beth arrived at the airport at 8:45 P.M. She received the promised text from Mancuso with all the details. She decided to dress casually for the flight. She wore jeans, a long-sleeved T-shirt, and comfortable shoes. Her shoulder-length blonde hair dried naturally after her recent bath since she didn't have time to dry and style it properly. Check-in and security clearance at the airport were both a breeze. Beth was familiar with the ropes since flying commercially in recent months, becoming comfortable with the routine, the arrival process, and boarding the plane.

She quickly found a vacant seat and waited patiently for the boarding announcement. As she waited, her mind flashed back to the life circumstances leading her to her current situation.

Immediately following her graduation, Beth eloped to Las Vegas with her childhood sweetheart, Mark White. He was older, having already obtained his license and working as a real estate agent.

Only a few months into their marriage, everyone was surprised when Beth announced her decision to join the military. An even bigger surprise than the initial one was her choice of field. She enlisted and trained in protective security services, which shocked those closest to her, given her calm demeanor and petite size.

This is when she met and was assigned to work with Sergeant Mancuso. He was patient with her as she learned the ropes and eagerly absorbed all his instructions. His belief in her pushed her to become the best recruit. She knew she would not be where she was today without him and his training.

While enlisted, she completed a master's degree in business, as well as a bachelor's degree in finance. After twelve years of service, she and Mark mutually decided she would not renew her enlistment. They felt it was time to move closer to family, planning to settle down in their hometown and prepare for their future, with the intention of having children.

Before long, they built a business and opened their own real estate agency. Mark, as the realtor, sold the houses, while Beth focused on all the paperwork concerning business and finances. Their system worked seamlessly.

Beth had a plan, and Mark could see their future as they envisioned it. Their perfect dream home came on the market, and they purchased it immediately. Everything was falling into place according to Beth's plan. They had built a solid foundation, deciding now was the perfect time to start a family. Life was great…until it wasn't.

Unexpectedly, both of Beth's parents passed away shortly after they moved home. They were soulmates, so it was no surprise they had both died within a couple of months of each other, both due to heart conditions. Beth was devastated, but she accepted her situation as a life lesson: life is short, and she should strive to live as healthy as possible. Although she wasn't a fan of working out in a gym, she decided to take up daily walking instead. She soon realized that walking provided her with the time to think and strategize. Beth knew without a doubt that she had made the right decision to come home and leave her security career behind. She never regretted her choice, because to her, family was more important.

With the massive loss of her parents, she turned all her focus on Mark and the future family they planned to create. Mark and their dreams became her top priority. They were both excited for this new chapter in their lives—only to be heartbroken after twelve months with still no pregnancy.

It was then that the next tragedy hit their life: Mark was diagnosed with stage IV cancer, with a low survival rate. After only a few months, Mark succumbed to his illness, leaving Beth broken and alone in their now-empty dream house.

That was two years ago. With her previous intention of "life is short and playing it safe," she threw caution to the wind and went back to what was familiar to her. This is when she was hired to work for Sammie.

Beth's thoughts were interrupted by the announcement that it was time for her to board the plane.

Once onboard, she glanced at her fellow passengers. The plane was only half full, as taking the red-eye flight was not for the faint of heart. The pilot's voice filled the cabin intercom, welcoming everyone aboard, even making a joke that he hoped he could stay awake. The flight attendants then provided safety instructions, and right on schedule Beth found herself in the air, heading toward Las Vegas.

The flight was not non-stop, as there was a brief stop in Michigan. Passengers traveling the distance to Las Vegas stayed on board, while a few others exited the plane. Minutes later, they were back in the air, now with two additional passengers on board.

Beth's mind raced with thoughts of what awaited her in Las Vegas. She had numerous unanswered questions swirling in her head. She replayed her conversation with Mancuso, trying to remember every word he had said. She wondered if he had offered any clues about this blind interview event. Her main concern was that she had never heard of such a thing before, leaving her to question whether it was real.

She did feel a sense of trust in the process, largely because Mancuso believed in both it and her capabilities. He was the only reason she had said yes to this opportunity, and why she was now venturing into unknown territory. Confusion and curiosity battled within her. One moment, she was excited about the spontaneous adventure; the next, she questioned why she had agreed to such an uncertain, last-minute interview, a process she knew absolutely nothing about, except that it was for a personal assistant position requiring security training.

Beth pondered whether her master's degree in business administration and her bachelor's degree in finance would be advantageous for the personal assistant role. However, without knowing the specifics of the position, she was unsure whether her educational background would truly be a good fit.

She had hoped to catch a few hours of sleep during the final leg of the flight, but now found herself wide awake, her racing thoughts preventing her from resting. As they approached Las Vegas, the excitement of the unknown added to her insomnia. Instead of sleeping, she decided to try resting her eyes practicing deep breathing relaxation techniques that she had learned during her training for situations where sleep was not an option. Her new focus was to appear rested and prepared for the unknown interview, rather than looking fatigued.

Frustrated that even her relaxation attempts were disrupted by wandering thoughts, she began to question whether she had made the right decision in accepting this last-minute offer. Although she was known for her willingness to embrace the unknown, she wondered if she was simply being foolish. The thought brought a smile to her face.

Interrupting her thoughts, the pilot's voice filled the cabin once again. He announced their pending arrival in Las Vegas, expressing pride in their punctuality as they would arrive ten minutes ahead of schedule.

Beth felt a sudden surge of energy. Although she thrived under pressure, she appreciated the extra minutes to navigate the airport. She smiled to herself, realizing she now had more time to prepare physically for the interview, with over an hour to spare before her car and driver were scheduled to arrive and pick her up.

CHAPTER THREE

It was 6:15 A.M. Friday, and Marcus couldn't sleep. His mind was preoccupied with the CV Mancuso had presented to him yesterday. He was still not convinced that B. White was the standout applicant, as suggested on paper. His trust in Mancuso assured him that he would not knowingly recommend someone with fraudulent information; he was sure of that. However, he couldn't fathom how someone with such a well-documented CV could still be in search of a high-profile position.

Yesterday, they had agreed that today's interview process needed to be unbiased. Therefore, they chose not to ask Mancuso for additional information, opting instead to trust the process. Now, after a restless night, he found himself wanting to know more. He decided to send Mancuso a brief text, simply confirming whether B. White was en route to Las Vegas. He needed to know if the applicant would be attending the interview event in the Number 10 position. Mancuso responded, assuring him that they were indeed on a plane, without providing further details, and Marcus accepted his response respectfully.

Marcus realized it wasn't fair to the other applicants for him to seek additional information, but his curiosity was piqued. He convinced himself it was merely a matter of potential fraud, nothing more. He felt he needed and wanted more information about this mysterious candidate. After some consideration, he decided to ask for Bobby's assistance; he trusted his instincts.

Marcus had a variety of drivers over the years, and he always hired them from the same agency. They would schedule whichever driver was available whenever he was in town. As he became more well-known and his security measures tightened, he was allowed to request specific drivers; this is how he met Bobby.

Before long, Bobby became his exclusive personal chauffeur and bodyguard. Having been through thick and thin together, their friendship evolved rapidly. Bobby quickly became one of Marcus's few true friends and his best companion.

Marcus felt fortunate to have Bobby, always ready to listen with an open ear and a kind heart, as they navigated many situations over the years. Bobby was honest and open about complex topics, and Marcus held the utmost respect for this gentle giant.

Marcus caved into his curiosity at 6:20 A.M., deciding to call Bobby. He reached for his phone, mentally preparing for the possibility that he might be waking him up. Still, he hoped Bobby would agree to help him with his unusual request, knowing he would understand once he explained his concerns.

***

Bobby Simmons had worked for Marcus for 18 years. Bobby's father was a chauffeur for the "pretty people," as he would jokingly refer to them. His dad was a freelance driver who never had an exclusive employment contract with a single celebrity. His reputation and income were built on his acceptance into select groups, and his availability increased as the industry expanded.

Many times, Bobby would don his Sunday best, wear one of his father's old chauffeur hats, and ride along, creating memories that would last a lifetime. As the demand for limo drivers grew in California, Bobby's dad felt like a small fish in a big pond. This prompted him to upgrade to a newer, more luxurious limousine, helping him remain popular and active in the increasingly competitive celebrity scene. Bobby never heard his father complain; he knew his dad was respected and had loyal connections that kept the bills paid.

Bobby was tall and lanky as a teenager, towering over most of his peers. When he entered high school, he began weight training with the goal of getting "buff." With dedication, he developed a passion for weightlifting and took pride in the transformation of his physique. By his senior year, Bobby was almost unrecognizable due to the significant changes in his body mass and size, having grown into a tall, solid man that no one would dare mess with.

However, before he could follow in his father's footsteps, tragedy struck. His father suffered a massive heart attack and passed away. With no life insurance and the burden of expenses, his mother made the difficult decision to sell the family-owned limousine.

Determined to honor his father's legacy, Bobby obtained his chauffeur's license after graduating. Unsurprisingly, thanks to being the son of a respected community member, he was welcomed and quickly hired. He enjoyed a few prosperous years driving, but soon noticed that the "pretty people," as his father had called them, were not as kind to drivers as he remembered them being with his dad.

His dedication to fitness and desire to remain within the celebrity circuit opened new doors for him. He enrolled in a police training course for non-police officers and graduated at the top of his class after twelve weeks, making him a highly sought-after candidate. It was then that he made a pivotal career choice, becoming a security guard, which secured him exclusive roles for several A-list celebrities and high-profile individuals. He was in high demand as he could perform the dual role of chauffeur and bodyguard. He met his wife, Chloe, during a dual role assignment. They married in Las Vegas and decided to call it home.

Soon, Marcus began requesting Bobby's services whenever he was in town. This marked the beginning of their unlikely, yet mutually respectful, friendship. Most of their private conversations consisted of Marcus asking Bobby about his life and his wife Chloe. Bobby soon realized that Marcus was trying to visualize what everyday life looked like through his eyes. They rarely discussed Marcus's own life, but when they did, Bobby could sense the sadness stemming from Marcus's self-isolation from the world. Bobby felt a deep sorrow for the most popular man in the world; all he wanted was to be left alone during his downtime and to lead a somewhat normal life with his family.

Their friendship grew, and both trusted that they could confide in each other, knowing their conversations would always remain private.

One momentous day, Bobby received a routine call for transport at the Donovan estate. Nothing out of the ordinary, as Marcus always requested Bobby when he was in town. When he arrived at the mansion, he recognized Rodney and Donald waiting outside. He knew them both from previous encounters.

"Good morning, Mr. Simmons. Mr. Donovan is requesting for you to join him inside. Please follow us."

Bobby followed the two men. He had always dreamed of seeing inside Marcus's mansion. Although they had become friends, they had never socialized outside of the limo. Marcus owned one of the largest and most beautiful mansions on the outskirts of Las Vegas, but there had never been a reason for Bobby to be invited inside.

Donald recognized the look of concern on Bobby's face when he checked his watch.

"Don't worry about the time; you have been booked for the entire day," he reassured him.

Still surprised and a bit confused, Bobby shrugged his shoulders, continuing to follow the men up the steps and through the massive door of the mansion. Stepping inside, he could hardly believe his eyes. He wasn't sure what he had expected, but this exceeded his wildest imagination.

The foyer was enormous, yet it didn't feel cold, as one might expect from such a large entrance. Instead, a warm and pleasant feeling enveloped him. His first thought was that it felt like Marcus—kind and welcoming. As he looked around, marveling at the beautiful mixture of warmth and elegance in the foyer, he spotted Marcus in another room.

When the trio entered the room, Marcus, who was sitting on one of the many beautiful couches, got to his feet and welcomed Bobby to his home. They greeted each other with a familiar handshake, or more of a "man shake"—a handshake accompanied by a one-arm side hug, a bro-hug.

That was eighteen years ago, the day Marcus chose Las Vegas as his permanent residence; the day Bobby became his exclusive driver and personal security bodyguard. It was the day they became confidants for each other, a sounding board for frustrations, and, at times, Bobby became Marcus's only solid voice of reason. It was the day they became trusted best friends.

***

Sleeping soundly next to Chloe, Bobby was awakened by the programmed ringtone and knew it was Marcus calling, even without looking at the phone.

Bobby knew Marcus well enough to realize that he would never call him on his day off unless it was something important. He answered with his eyes still closed, not bothering to disguise his groggy, sleepy voice.

"Hey boss," he said.

Marcus began speaking immediately, aware that time was of the essence.

"Hi Bobby, I'm really sorry to call you so early and wake you, but I have a situation that I only trust you with."

"Sure, what's up?"

"I hate to disturb you on your day off. Especially since I was the one who stressed how important it was to take it, almost to the point of forcing you. Something has come up, and I need your help for the entire day. I promise I will make it up to you. Can you change your plans?"

Noticing the anxious tone in Marcus's voice, Bobby decided to lighten the mood with a bit of humor.

"Sure boss. I was just going to do a few things around the house, mostly just relaxing actually. In case you didn't know, my boss can be such a beast to work for."

He sensed Marcus's laugh on the other end, and he smiled, loving the opportunity to make him laugh. Given the demands placed on him, Bobby often wondered how Marcus managed to get through most days.

Marcus began speaking rapidly, briefly explaining a last-minute addition to today's blind interview event. He sounded frustrated as he bombarded Bobby with a series of disjointed statements about the late arrival of the tenth applicant. Marcus was clearly rambling.

"B. White must be picked up from the airport no later than 8:00 A.M. The flight is scheduled to arrive at 7:00 A.M. The allotted arrival time at the event center is 10:45 A.M."

Confused by this chaotic conversation, Bobby rubbed his eyes as he got out of bed and went into the kitchen. He was trying to process the rapid-fire information from Marcus. He knew Marcus was anxious about the position. However, he did not understand what made it so urgent that he only trusted him to help. Once again, he decided to tease Marcus a little.

"I'm glad to help you man, but I must have missed the part where this became urgent, and you could only trust me with a routine airport pickup."

Only then did Marcus realize how outlandish and vague his request had sounded.

"Bobby, I'm sorry. In my rush and word vomit, I skipped some important parts of my concern. In hindsight, I guess my request did sound a bit strange, even for me."

They both laughed, and Bobby could hear Marcus take a deep breath, trying to calm down and speak more slowly.

"I am concerned about the character of this applicant. The CV looks almost too good to be true. I am worried it might be fake or exaggerated. I need to gather more information about them before the interview to assess their character. I need your thoughts on this."

Intrigued, Bobby asked how Marcus had obtained this mysterious CV for B. White, the tenth applicant, in the first place. He could hear a rare tone of frustration building in Marcus's voice.

"Mancuso had this CV. He provided it to the team when we were short on applicants. Since when does Mancuso carry a CV in his pocket? You know I trust Mancuso completely, but I fear there might be deceit on the applicant's part. I cannot shake this sinking feeling in my stomach. Something feels off about this candidate. If they are such an outstanding asset, why aren't they already under contract?"

Without needing to say a word, they both knew Marcus wanted Bobby to reassure him of his trust in Mancuso, which Bobby gladly did.

"Boss man we both know you can trust Mancuso. So, if this applicant is fraudulent, he likely doesn't know it. How can I help? What do you need me to do?"

Marcus was relieved Bobby didn't dismiss his concerns as paranoia. The problem now was, he was not exactly sure what he wanted Bobby to do. He had not thought that far ahead before making the call; he was just winging it.

"This is why I called you. We need to gather more information before the event. Mainly, I need your insight on this candidate. Perhaps you could wear your hat camera. I feel the need to observe their normal behavior outside of the interview. I know it sounds over the top, even for me, but I need to know if this CV is genuine. I do not have time to be scammed."

Sensing Marcus's aggravation beginning to build again, which was unusual for him, Bobby saw an opportunity to lighten the tense atmosphere once again.

"Not everyone is out to get you, Mr. Big Shot."

Marcus recognized exactly what Bobby's intent was, and it helped ease his tension. Thinking this was the end of the call, he was surprised when Marcus continued speaking, making one final request.

"One last thing: use the limo cameras to record the ride to the event center. I want to cover all my bases. Normally, I would be against spying on someone, but for some reason, this situation feels off to me."

Bobby knew what Marcus said was true. The industry had changed him; his trust had been broken more than once. Unfortunately, Marcus had encountered a significant amount of deception throughout his career. For his peace of mind, they both knew he needed to assess the accuracy of this candidate.

This request brought unease to Bobby, prompting him to wonder what was in the candidate's CV. Something must have raised major red flags.

"Got it! I look forward to meeting this mysterious candidate, B. White, and reviewing their CV. Consider this handled boss. I will do this for you. I will go and pick up candidate B. White from the airport and deliver them to the event by 10:30 A.M. for a 10:45 A.M. time slot. I promise you we will uncover whether B. White submitted fraudulent information to get this interview with you."

Marcus knew Bobby meant every word. Bobby had become very protective of him over the years, not just as an employee but also as a friend, a brother of sorts… family.

"I knew I could count on you my friend. Once again I apologize for calling you in on your day off. I promise I will make it up to you. Give Chloe my love and tell her I am sorry for stealing you away from her today."

Bobby smiled, confident that Marcus would indeed make it up to him, and then some.

"I will always have your back... but you're on your own with Chloe."

"You seem to forget that she loves me and has forgiven me before, but I promise to plan something special for you both when all this is over."

Bobby took a quick shower, got dressed, grabbed a couple of protein bars and a cup of coffee, kissed his beautiful wife, and headed out the door. Grateful for their home's close proximity to the airport, he arrived right at 7 A.M. He was on a mission, a mission to protect Marcus and to expose this potential fraud. The sooner he uncovered the truth about B. White, the better; it would save them all a considerable amount of time.

At 7:05 A.M., Bobby stood tall and rigid near the baggage claim, holding a sign that read "B. White." Uncertain about B. White's point of arrival or what they looked like, he continually scanned the crowd. As passengers passed by, he focused primarily on those dressed in business attire. He assumed that, given the tight timeline, the applicant would be prepared for an interview and dressed appropriately.

***

After landing, Beth grabbed her carry-on and made her way off the plane. She had a plan, as she always did. During the flight, she decided to go directly to the baggage carousel and then find the nearest women's restroom to change into her interview suit. There would be plenty of time to touch up her makeup, and she needed to do something about her air-dried hair, which seemed to have taken on a mind of its own since last night.

By her calculations, after navigating the airport to retrieve her luggage, she would have approximately 30 minutes to prepare to meet the car and driver, still arriving 15 minutes early.

Beth stepped off the escalator and noticed a neatly dressed, well-built middle-aged man. He undeniably looked like a chauffeur; she recognized the stance, making it easy to identify him among the crowd. She then saw he was holding a sign that read: "B. White."

Her mind raced. Her pickup driver was an hour early. She wasn't appropriately dressed for the interview. Taking a deep breath, she smiled at the driver and waved as she approached him.

"Hi, you must be here for me. I am B. White."

It would be an understatement to say Bobby was taken aback when a petite blonde in jeans and a T-shirt approached him, claiming to be B. White. He immediately thought she had wasted everyone's time and money by attending this high-profile interview event. Marcus's instinct that her CV was fraudulent, suggesting it looked "loaded and padded" on paper, seemed correct. Given her appearance, Bobby was astonished her CV had even made it onto the list of today's interviewees. He then recalled she was added as a favor to Mancuso, also filling the vacant spot of the tenth candidate.

He smiled, trying his best to hide his concerns and unsure of what to say next. As she stopped in front of him, extending her hand, he could not mask his surprise, although he tried.

Beth noticed his disbelief but continued to smile, attempting to sound cheerful.

"Well now, aren't you the early bird?"

"Always," he replied.

The driver chuckled slightly as he noticed her faint southern twang. He shook the tiny hand she offered. He appreciated her attitude; he had to give her that much. He excelled at reading expressions and could tell her mind was briefly whirling. However, her smile and pleasant demeanor never faltered. Shockingly, he was impressed. Before he had time to fully process their situation, she began giving him directions with precise authority.

"This is great, you just added a few extra minutes to my timeline. Could you please go and retrieve my luggage from baggage claim? While you do that, I will head to the women's restroom to get ready."

Seeing the look of concern on his face, the look men give women when they suspect getting ready will take forever, she quickly reassured him.

"Don't worry, I won't be long. I am always prepared. By the way, you cannot miss my luggage. It is white with green and black swirls and has a pink ribbon tied to the handle. I'll be back in a jiffy, fifteen minutes tops."

Her voice was sweet but not bossy; it was, however, authoritative and to the point.

Caught slightly off guard, and before Bobby could fully grasp the situation with this unexpected interaction, she had arranged for him to retrieve her luggage from the baggage carousel. The driver had no verbal response, only a slight smile on his face as Beth turned quickly to dart into the crowd, making her way to the women's restroom. She stopped mid-stride and turned back to face him.

"I am sorry hon I didn't ask. What is your name, sir?"

"Bobby."

"Nice to meet you Bobby, I'm Beth."

With that, she disappeared among the multitude of people in the airport, heading for the nearest women's room.

Bobby made his way to the carousel as she directed him, ready to retrieve the white, green, and black piece of luggage with a pink ribbon. He tried to wrap his mind around what had just happened. He smiled, realizing being caught off guard was not something that normally happened to him. Still, he thought she certainly did not fit the mold of someone applying for a position as an assistant/security guard to an international icon. Then he remembered this was an anonymous interview; she had no idea who the available position was for. He muttered to himself, shaking his head.

"Marcus, you may have gotten this one right buddy."

As he stood patiently waiting for the luggage belt to begin, Bobby's mind drifted to his current situation: waiting in an airport for an unknown woman who was changing her clothes. After many years of marriage, he shook his head, thinking,

"We will never make our designated time slot."

He checked his watch, hoping she didn't take too long in the women's restroom, as they were on a tight schedule. Again, he worried they would surely miss the arrival time, which he found unacceptable. He began to consider the option of directing her to stay at the airport for her return flight, as she would not be allowed to attend the event if she arrived late.

***

Once in the restroom, Beth took a moment to assess her situation. Since her interview attire was in her luggage and the chauffeur had arrived early, she needed to implement her Plan B. Plan B was an alternate interview outfit. She refused to panic; she always had a backup plan for situations like this. Plan B kept her prepared in case her luggage got lost or, in this case, when she couldn't retrieve it on time. However, her Plan

B wasn't a business suit, nor was it the jeans and T-shirt she had worn for the last eight and a half hours of traveling.

Beth quickly found an empty stall and changed into a pair of black slim-cut ankle-length dress pants, a white tank top, and a white oversized high-low cotton shirt, paired with black flats. She washed her face and reapplied her foundation, mascara, and neutral lipstick. Given her tight timeline, she decided to put her hair up, leaving the tousled ends to fall loosely over her head. It was the best she could do given her new shorter agenda.

Looking at her watch, she realized she had been away from Bobby for almost 15 minutes. She gave herself one last look in the mirror and decided to add a touch of blush to give her neutral look a bit of color. After a final glance and a quick nod of approval, she left the restroom and made her way towards the baggage claim. From a distance, she saw Bobby retrieving her luggage from the carousel. Taking a breath, Beth smiled, pleased with her initial calculations. In her original plan, she had allocated 15 minutes for retrieving her luggage.

Bobby found her suitcase just as she had described. As he looked up, he saw Beth heading towards him. With a quick glance at the time, he noticed it was almost 7:25 A.M., and B. White had been gone for the full 15 minutes.

"Well I'll be damned. I would have lost money on that bet."

He was impressed and noticed she was still smiling. Bobby studied the young woman in black and white as she approached him. Honestly, he was surprised she wasn't wearing what most would consider appropriate attire for such a high-profile interview event. However, he had to admit she still looked professional and somewhat classic. He couldn't help but think about how unique she was. She walked with assurance and confidence, and since meeting her, he'd noticed she had been kind, with a smile that never faltered.

Beth's smile widened as she stopped beside Bobby, trying to read his expression, which she found difficult. The first thought crossing her mind was that he did not believe she would return this soon, but he chose not to mention it.

"See, I knew you would know which suitcase was mine. Easy peasy huh?"

CHAPTER FOUR

Marcus arrives at the event center at 8:00 A.M., before the first candidate, who is scheduled for 8:30 A.M. All ten CVs are neatly arranged on a large desk in time order, waiting for the arrival of Maggie, the receptionist.

Each chauffeur has been given the name and contact information of their interviewee, as well as the time they are allowed to enter the building. They will receive two text messages when it is their candidate's entrance time: one five minutes before the scheduled time, and another one minute before. When the interviewee enters, they will be greeted by Maggie, a sweet receptionist. She has been instructed to be friendly and polite, engaging each applicant in pleasant conversation. Marcus also requested that she portray a woman with extreme underlying stress and possible sadness, while still remaining professional.

Marcus's number one attribute in any person is kindness and compassion. He needs to witness each applicant's reaction to Maggie's behavior—her subtle signs of being overwhelmed and stressed.

He settles down behind the two-way mirror, watching the waiting room, and preparing for what he expects to be a long and hopefully productive day. The event center has cameras located at the entrance door, as well as at Maggie's desk.

With a quick glance at the clock, Marcus sees it is now 8:25 A.M. Taking a deep breath, he exhales, then begins to review the day's agenda with his team.

"Okay guys, we have two and a half hours to watch these candidates' behaviors and interactions. We will break from

11:00 A.M. to 12:00 P.M. for lunch. We will then have a team discussion about what we have learned about our candidates. Hopefully, we will have a great idea of who our top candidates are. At 12:10 P.M., Rodney will announce the decision of our first cut."

He notices the concerned look on the faces of his team and feels the need to justify his decision to make the cut so soon.

"I know you have mixed thoughts about this plan; however, I believe it is best to do the cut before the real-life exercise. Otherwise, this process drags out, and the candidates get annoyed. The real-life exercise lasts thirty to forty-five minutes each, depending on the applicant's performance. When all the exercises are completed, the applicants will be notified to expect a call within twenty-four hours if they are chosen. I don't want to make any hasty decisions. The other nine will receive an email thanking them for their time and attendance today."

Rodney is the only one to speak out against Marcus's plan.

"Do you think it's fair to cut the applicants based on their appearance? We have already viewed their CVs."

The room goes quiet, each person looking to the other for additional input.

"I hear you Rodney. I am not looking solely at appearance, but I want to feel a connection—a vibe if you will. I also have a plan to see behaviors, things we couldn't see on the CV."

The room is still quiet, but each of them eventually nods in agreement with Marcus's reasoning.

The process begins promptly at 8:30 A.M., with each applicant entering the building at their designated times.

As he watches, Marcus's first thought is that they look as though they have gone shopping together. They are all dressed alike—very professional—but all wearing gray suits. Even the women are wearing gray suits. He also notices each of them carrying a briefcase, which he finds interesting since he already has their CVs.

Chuckling to himself, he wonders if it is part of the ensemble, perhaps a briefcase was included with the purchase of the suit.

He then returns his focus to the interviewees. Marcus tries to remain positive; after all, he isn't sure what he expected them to look like. This is an interview, and each of the applicants is dressed accordingly. Suits are considered professional attire for a job interview. He decides to dismiss their attire, yet he still feels underwhelmed by what he has witnessed today.

More importantly, other than the polite exchange expected at an interview, he has yet to see any of the candidates truly engage with Maggie.

Applicant number nine now enters the building. Again, another gray suit. By this point, Marcus is bored and disappointed. He had expected to feel an instant connection when the right applicant arrived. Instead, he finds himself returning to the CVs, trying to read between the lines to see if the perfect applicant is possibly among today's group. He cringes at the thought of enduring another full day of interviews.

***

"So, where do we go from here to get to your car?"

With her luggage in hand, Beth follows Bobby as he leads her toward a private parking area where the limo is waiting. He loads her luggage, and as he closes the trunk, he notices she has opened the front passenger door.

"Shotgun."

She hops in, closing the door behind her. When he enters the driver's seat, she is laughing—a genuine belly laugh. Smiling at her, he shakes his head slightly, thinking this will be an enjoyable day, a story to remember. Now he is laughing too, realizing he may have misjudged her.

He suddenly recognizes that he likes this girl after all. Beth is different—genuinely friendly and a breath of fresh air in the stuffy world he is used to. He finds himself secretly hoping she has not falsified her CV. He has a feeling she might be the perfect person for Marcus.

Since he now decides he likes her, his brow furrows, and he immediately worries that this interview might break her kind spirit. Beth notices the slight frown on his face and misinterprets it as a reaction to her riding in the front seat.

"Was that too forward of me? I'm so sorry. I should have asked, not assumed it was okay to ride in the front."

"No you're fine in the front seat. I was just thinking I'd hate to see Las Vegas change you. It tends to do that to most people—and not always in a good way."

Giving him another one of her genuine smiles, along with a lighthearted wink, Beth replies,

"Thank you for your concern Bobby, but I'm a lot tougher than I look. I'm known to be unbreakable and have been exposed to more than most. I got this."

"Okay. Just be careful, please."

"Aye Aye Captain. Thanks."

Bobby navigates the limo out of the parking area. Beth, eager to obtain any information Mancuso may not have shared, begins to fire questions at him.

"So, how far do we have to go to this event thingy?"

Her casual question surprises Bobby, making him laugh again. She appears so unsuspecting and carefree. He wonders if she has any idea of the status and caliber of the people she could encounter today—or maybe she does, and it doesn't matter to her.

"Not too far. It's outside the city limits, about thirty minutes or so."

Beth decides now is the best time to strike up a conversation.

"What do you know about this event? How much can you tell me?"

He soon realizes Beth has more questions than he has answers, and she isn't shy about asking for as much information as he can provide. Her questions are both professional and personal, but none are inappropriate or rude. Bobby navigates the busy traffic seamlessly, answering Beth's questions as best as he can.

"It's my understanding there will be ten applicants today. I was told you were a last-minute add-on, which makes you the tenth. Each interviewee is scheduled fifteen minutes apart from the others. They call it a blind interview event, meaning none of the ten applicants know the potential employer. The potential employer could be a celebrity, a millionaire, or a politician—it's unknown at the time of the event. Sometimes the potential employer is on-site, but most times the event is overseen by their representatives."

She feels disappointed with his responses, which are only slightly more detailed than what Mancuso had shared. By Bobby's general answers, she surmises that he is as in the dark as she is; after all, he's only the chauffeur.

Seeing the mixed look of disappointment and frustration on her face at not receiving in-depth information, Bobby takes the opportunity to change the subject, turning the questions toward her.

"So, enlighten me—how did you end up here today?"

"I received a call last night with an invitation to attend. Now here I am, fifteen hours later, in Las Vegas."

Her answer is short and sweet, and Bobby is slightly in awe that she is so adventurous. Maybe there is more to her than the lovely girl who got off that plane in jeans and a T-shirt.

Her responses intrigue him, making him want to hear more. She is inquisitive and straightforward. He is impressed by her positive and professional attitude. He continues with the most obvious question.

"So, you dropped everything to jump on a plane, at the last minute, for a position you know nothing about?"

"Yep. I let my curiosity and the promise of an unknown adventure get the best of me every time. Most times it works out."

She finds Bobby easy to talk to and soon shares her personal story before realizing it.

"I was young when I joined the military. My family was surprised—actually shocked—to learn my training was in special protective services. When I chose not to re-enlist, my husband and I moved home and opened a family real estate business. Sadly, our dream didn't last long. My husband was diagnosed with cancer, and it stole him away from us."

"Anyway, my last assignment was with a rising pop star. She is nice but young and loves the limelight. The position was more like babysitting, so it was uneventful. Honestly, even without the excitement, the position helped to fill the void of loneliness."

She watches Bobby's face as she speaks and can tell from his expression that he was not expecting—or possibly even believing—everything she just told him.

"Sorry for the overload of unsolicited information. I tend to ramble sometimes."

"No. Thank you for sharing. It sounds like you've dealt with a lot of tough times in your life. Maybe today will be the beginning of a new adventure."

"Maybe. I'll cross my fingers."

Traffic in Las Vegas is busier than normal, so the commute to the event center takes a little longer than usual. Bobby always anticipates the worst-case scenario when it comes to traffic, hence his early arrival at the airport. He now finds he doesn't mind spending a few extra minutes getting to know Beth. She seems kind, friendly, and talented. Could she be the one?

Bobby is known for his exceptional talent at reading first impressions, and Marcus is well aware of this. That's why he asked Bobby to be the one transporting this interviewee. Beth may not have passed his first impression, but she has surpassed his second with flying colors.

As he listens to her describe her career, family, and lost dreams, he realizes he knows exactly why she was invited to this event. From what he has learned about her in such a short time, she may even be overqualified for the role of personal assistant, even with the added security aspect.

The car slows as they approach an older one-story building on the outskirts of town. It's large and made of brick, but not overly extravagant. Nothing about the building designates it as a high-profile event center. Off the beaten path, it looks plain and boring—like any other in the area.

She notices there are nine limos already parked out front; theirs makes the tenth. She feels a mixture of puzzlement and anticipation.

"This is it? This is the secret location?"

Her eyes search the area intently, but she sees no distinctive signs on the building.

For the first time since meeting her, Bobby notices she's not smiling. He hears the shift in her tone and knows she is unsure. She's in disbelief that someone so important would be in such a bland, nondescript location. Pulling into the parking lot, he quickly reassures her.

"Yep, this is the place. I know it doesn't look like much, but it's the real deal."

He parks the limo and checks his watch. It's time to let Marcus know they've arrived.

He sends Marcus a text: "B. White has arrived. We are in the parking lot at the event center. :)."

He adds a smile emoji simply because he can't help himself. Smiling, he places his phone back in the console.

"Okay Beth, we have thirty minutes before your designated time to enter."

She's still focused on the building, searching for anything to reassure her that this last-minute adventure isn't a scam. She's sure Bobby recognizes her concern.

He studies the look on her face; even though he has only just met her, he feels the need to give her a little pep talk.

"Can I give you some unsolicited advice?"

She nods toward him to continue.

"Beth, trust me, this is a genuine, honest interview. This process is real. Big-name people do these types of things all the time. Yes, I know it sounds unbelievable and surreal, but the main thing is for you to go in there and be yourself. This is a once-in-a-lifetime experience. After only just meeting you, it's apparent to me that you have significant knowledge and training, qualifying you for this—or any other—position."

She wants to trust him; his voice sounds sincere. She has come this far, and she isn't about to bail out now. She has never run from the unknown, and she isn't starting today.

"Thanks for your kind words and for reminding me to trust those around me. I know Mancuso would have never added me to the mix if this weren't the real deal."

"Exactly! Let me reiterate—you need to be at your best to make the cut. It can and will get brutal in there."

"Yay! Finally something familiar. I thrive on the brutal stuff."

They both laugh, and Beth takes a deep breath, relaxing slightly.

Bobby decides to change the subject, engaging her in easy, random conversation to pass the time as they wait for her designated slot.

At 10:40 A.M., Rodney sends Bobby a text. It simply reads:

"Prepare to send in number ten, 10:45 A.M."

When the text comes, Bobby gives Beth one last pep talk before she exits the car.

"I know we only met two and a half hours ago, but it's clear to me that you're more than qualified. You'll excel if you're chosen for this position. They'll be lucky to have you on their team—I know I would.

"My last piece of advice: walk into that building like a boss. You deserve to be here. You're efficient, organized, you know how to take charge, and you're confident. Add in your smile and friendliness, and you'll always achieve positive results."

His sincerity shocks her. She has only just met him, and yet he has such kind words about her—it's a huge compliment. Before she can respond, Bobby's phone pings again. This time the text contains only the time: 10:44 A.M.

Their eyes meet.

"Okay Beth. Show time. Be yourself—and show them what they'll be missing if you don't make the cut. Good luck."

Beth flashes her million-dollar smile at Bobby.

"Thanks, Bobby, for your kind words—and thanks for the pep talk. You're right. I'll just be me, and the rest is on them."

She gives him a high five. As she closes the door, she pauses to ask if she'll be returning to his car when this is all over. He gives a slight nod with a short reply.

"Most definitely."

As she approaches the door, she turns back, giving him one last smile and a small nod before disappearing inside the building.

Bobby thinks to himself, "Damn right I'll be here." He's already eager to hear how this unlikely candidate fares today.

He isn't sure why—since they've only just met—but Bobby has a gut feeling that Beth might do exceptionally well.

CHAPTER FIVE

Beth enters the unmarked office building, stepping into a large waiting room. She notices a receptionist seated at a desk on the far side of the room. As she starts across the room, she observes the other nine applicants already seated around tables, waiting. They are all dressed in classic gray business attire, with briefcases placed beside them on the floor, next to their expensive shoes. For a moment, Beth feels uneasy about her outfit, wishing she had packed a suit in her carry-on as a backup. Oh well, nothing she can do about it now. Bobby's words come to mind: "Walk in like a boss." That is precisely what she does. If she is going to stand out, it won't be because she isn't wearing a business suit and expensive shoes. With her head held high and posture erect, she continues to stride confidently across the room to greet the receptionist.

***

Marcus feels defeated, as not a single candidate has visibly impressed him today. He is beginning to believe the day will be a bust, as he still hasn't seen a standout. He isn't sure exactly what he expected, but none of the candidates made him take a second look. He now waits for the tenth applicant. Bobby sent a notification of their arrival via text, but Marcus doesn't understand the emoji. This piques his curiosity. He expects another gray suit and briefcase to walk through the door. Marcus and his team watch from behind the two-way mirror as the door opens, and a petite blonde wearing an oversized white shirt, black fitted dress pants, and black flats enters. Her smile lights up the entire room.

They are silent in the quiet of the room. You can hear Rodney take a sharp breath. Marcus bursts out laughing.

"B. White is a woman! This is definitely not what I expected. She's unlike the other cookie-cutter applicants—not another gray suit with a briefcase. I still have reservations about the legitimacy of her CV, but I'm now more eager to see if she's as extraordinary as portrayed."

Suddenly, he realizes Bobby's reason for the smiley emoji and smiles, thinking of his friend.

"He could have just told me, but no, he's probably enjoying my shock far more than he should."

Marcus smiles, aware his friend is likely feeling particularly proud of himself at this moment. He returns his attention to number ten, watching as she glances around the room. For a second, he thinks he notices a hint of uneasiness or discomfort in her eyes, but it quickly vanishes. She walks confidently toward the receptionist.

Beth approaches Maggie, the receptionist, and notices her furrowed brow and slight frown; she looks sad.

"Good morning! I hope your day hasn't been too stressful."

The receptionist flashes a small, forced smile. In a whispered tone, she responds to Beth's concern.

"Good morning. I'm okay, maybe just a little stressed. The tension in here makes me uncomfortable. I'm sorry; I shouldn't have said anything."

Beth gives her a slight wink and a sincere smile.

"No worries sweetie! Your secret's safe with me. This is just a little girl talk, okay? So, last but not least, I'm your number ten, B. White."

The receptionist looks pleased and slightly amused. Maggie returns Beth's warm smile as she reaches for the folder labeled "B. White" on her desk and hands it to her. She provides Beth with completion instructions and directs her to the only empty seat at the table.

"Thanks sweetie. Look at that beautiful smile—you wear it well. It's just a job, shug; don't let it steal your beauty."

"Ms. White, it's been my pleasure to assist you."

Marcus watches the interaction between B. White and Maggie intently, noting the flash of concern and empathy on

B. White's face as the two women converse. Number ten places her hand on Maggie's and offers what appears to be words of encouragement. This is the kind of exchange Marcus has been waiting to witness all day, but none of the previous nine interviewees displayed it.

Beth takes the folder and makes her way to the vacant chair at the table, as Maggie instructed. She feels the eyes of the other interviewees following her. She pretends not to notice the stares, but her training has taught her to always be aware of her surroundings and the behaviors of those around her.

Maintaining a friendly smile, she greets the person seated across from her as she takes her seat. She silently reminds herself to keep her head high and stay professional; she is more than qualified to be here.

As she reviews the contents of the folder, she's surprised to see her current CV along with a written letter of recommendation from Mancuso. She briefly scans the document, shakes her head, and thinks, "Of course you added your opinion in letter form."

Once she has reviewed and signed the paperwork, the receptionist comes over to the table to retrieve it. They exchange smiles as Maggie whispers, "Good luck."

Maggie walks away, taking Beth's folder through a door at the back of the room. Now, Beth waits—they all wait. Once again, she notices the stares from her surroundings, but unphased, she remains confident, knowing that if given the chance, she will prove why she was invited. For now, her sole focus is on making the first cut.

Marcus observes B. White as she genuinely smiles at those who make eye contact upon taking her seat at the table. He notices that while a couple of the interviewees smile back, most don't. He makes a note of these reactions beside their names, marking them as an adverse response to kindness.

Then, he scans the room for other signs of negativity and is surprised to see that at least two interviewees seem to be judging Number Ten's relaxed yet professional appearance. He documents this observation as a negative response beside their names as well.

Promptly at 11:00 A.M., Maggie stands confidently before the ten interviewees.

"Thank you all for joining us today. In a few minutes, a member of the prospective employer's team will welcome you and provide further instructions. Please be patient as you wait."

Still curious about the secrecy surrounding the event, Beth decides to strike up a conversation with those sitting nearby.

Marcus continues to observe the behavior of the interviewees. Everyone is sitting quietly except B. White, who is whispering to the table next to hers. She asks them questions, and he notices they appear annoyed by her, responding in a blunt manner. Only one of the other applicants seems willing to converse briefly with her. Despite the cold atmosphere, only a morgue could match this room's stillness— she continues to smile warmly and offers a blanket apology for her intrusion.

Right on schedule, at 11:15 A.M., Rodney addresses the small group through the overhead intercom.

"Welcome everyone. We want to thank you all for attending on such short notice. The information you provided today is significant, and it will take my team and me some time to review. We will make our first cut after each folder has been thoroughly reviewed. This process is expected to take approximately one hour. Please take this opportunity to greet each other, get some fresh air, and enjoy the salad we have provided for lunch. We will resume and announce the first cut at 12:30 P.M."

The room collectively sighs with relief as the young man sitting across from Beth resumes their earlier conversation.

"Whew, that was short and to the point. I've attended one of these events before, but each one is unique. See those cameras? The potential employer might not even be on-site; they could be watching from another location."

"Either way is fine with me; they can watch me from wherever they want. I'm just hoping for a positive outcome. If not, there will be other assignments."

She then excuses herself to get some air, as the announcer recommended.

***

Marcus scans the room again to observe the candidates' reactions to Rodney's announcement. He is saddened to see no interaction among them, except for Number Ten.

Marcus has many questions and is eager to talk with Bobby, but he knows it's only fair to all the applicants to wait until after the first cut. He understands the importance of forming his own opinion before seeking Bobby's perspective. After all, he is there to choose the best person for the role of his personal/security assistant. However, he is intrigued and wants to know more about this Number Ten, whom Mancuso added at the last minute. Fighting his instinct to wait, he decides to call Bobby.

Bobby is laughing when he answers on the first ring, prompting a smile from Marcus.

"We'll discuss this later buddy. Right now, I need the Hat Cam SD card footage. I want to review it now."

They both know his review is not for interview purposes but out of curiosity.

"I already handed it off to Maggie boss. She should have placed it in the file. I knew you'd want to see it after you saw her."

Bobby chuckles as he pictures Marcus' reaction to the footage. He wishes he could be in the room to witness it firsthand, but his instructions for the day require him to stay with the car.

Marcus tries to sound stern.

"I can't with you right now, but trust me, we will discuss this later buddy."

He can only shake his head at Bobby's continued laughter.

"Thank you for once again anticipating my need to review it. Keep laughing, we will talk later."

He hangs up abruptly. Bobby still amused, knows Marcus well enough not to take it personally, understanding his curiosity.

Next on Marcus's agenda is Mancuso.

"Someone get Tony in here! I want to see him now—like five minutes ago!"

While he waits for Mancuso to arrive, Marcus asks Rodney to log in to the limo camera system so he can review the footage on his laptop. As Rodney completes this task, Marcus opens B. White's folder and discovers an SD card from Bobby's hat cam. He had initially missed it, as he hadn't opened her file today. He reviewed her CV yesterday, scrutinizing it for inconsistencies, and knew she hadn't added anything other than contact information today. In his defense, her folder was the last one received before the break announcement.

As he picks up the SD card, he can't help but smile, thinking about his friend.

"So you think you're the funny guy, huh? You think you know me, huh?" he says, addressing Bobby even though he isn't in the room.

He inserts the card and presses play on the laptop. Marcus finds himself unusually impatient when it takes longer than expected to load. He is eager to learn more about this mysterious woman.

Just then, a brief knock sounds at the door, and Mancuso walks in. Their eyes meet.

"Why didn't you tell me B. White was a woman?" Marcus asks.

Mancuso, anticipating being summoned, is not surprised by Marcus's agitated tone. He grins as he shrugs his shoulders.

"You didn't tell me the position was gender-specific. Is she not what you're looking for?" he replies, noticing the hat cam footage loading on the computer screen.

"What are you watching, and what exactly are you looking for?" Mancuso inquires.

"I want to see for myself what she's all about. Pull up a chair; I know you want to see it too."

"I know what she's about; I'm more curious to watch your reactions to White than to see her behavior myself. Remember, I know her."

Marcus fast-forwards through some of the footage due to time constraints, missing the initial interaction between Bobby and B. White. He misses her arrival, dressed casually in a T-shirt and jeans. When they resume watching, Marcus is surprised by her relaxed appearance. They observe her interaction with Bobby as she takes control of the luggage.

"Look at how she arranges for Bobby to retrieve her luggage. I want to skip ahead to her return."

He fast-forwards again, almost missing her return. Noting the timestamp, she had transformed into Number Ten, who entered the interview, in less than fifteen minutes. She is still smiling.

"Bobby sounds like he's warming up to her, even sounding a bit impressed. Look at the ease with which they exchange small talk on the way to the limo," Marcus notes.

Rodney and Donald have now joined the viewing party. They watch as her luggage is loaded into the limo, imagining Bobby's expression as she says "shotgun" and hops into the front passenger seat.

Mancuso, silently enjoying watching the others observe her, can no longer hold in his laughter.

"That's my girl. She's a force, for sure."

Marcus glares at his friend and laughs.

"You're truly enjoying this, aren't you Tony? You and Bobby both have jokes today, huh?"

Now the entire room breaks into laughter. Marcus has seen enough of this recording and switches to the limo camera footage. The coverage is vague, almost nonexistent, as B. White isn't riding in the back as anticipated. However, she can be heard discussing the event with Bobby.

Marcus listens to their interactions from the limo for a couple of minutes and realizes she is a genuinely kind person. However, this doesn't quell his concerns about her CV. You can be a nice person and still lie on a job application. Having seen enough, he shuts off the recording.

"Okay guys, we have nine more candidates to discuss before making our decision, and our time is ticking. You know I like to stay on schedule."

"Marcus, remember we don't have to make a final decision until after the exercise, or even tomorrow."

"That's true, Rodney, but I plan to weed out as many as possible before the exercise. We need to trust our instincts and follow our gut. I want someone nice and friendly. I choose those qualities over someone who's only good at their job but not naturally friendly."

"I need to feel a personal connection. Please understand my concerns."

His mind wanders to Number Ten, wondering if she could be both. He catches himself silently hoping she's not as fake as he initially thought.

CHAPTER SIX

While waiting for the results of the first cut, salads are offered for lunch. When Beth sees the food, she realizes how hungry she is. However, more than food, she craves caffeine. Her lack of sleep, combined with her empty stomach, is beginning to take a toll on her. She quickly grabs a salad and a soda from the small table and returns to her seat. After only a few bites of salad, her appetite has already diminished. She's not surprised; she often doesn't eat when she works and figures her body thinks this is just another workday.

However, she finishes the sweet, dark soda packed with caffeine. She gives herself a mental pep talk, reminding herself that she has come too far to give up now. A glance at her watch reveals she has about fifteen minutes left before she needs to be seated for the announcement of the results.

Deciding to take the announcer's advice, she walks outside for some fresh air. As she opens the door, a wall of dry heat immediately reminds her how quickly the temperature rises in Las Vegas.

Her mind briefly shifts to memories of the multiple trips she has taken to Las Vegas with Mark. This was their place. Their first visit was when they eloped, and since getting married, they have spent several anniversaries revisiting. They both enjoyed the city's energy at night, particularly the shows and strolling along the Strip.

Forcing her mind back to her current situation, Beth notices Bobby standing by his car. He's engaged in friendly conversation with the other drivers. When they hear the building door shut, all eyes in the parking lot turn toward her. Bobby flashes an inquisitive grin her way, and she gives him a quick thumbs-up. She then waves to the group of drivers before re-entering the building.

Once back in the cool room, Beth has no desire to finish eating her salad. She knows she should eat but also realizes she needs more energy than a salad can provide. She remembers the candy she packed in her bag for the flight—her sugar treats, which she always keeps on hand for situations like this. She finds the sought-after candy and hopes it will give her the quick energy boost she needs for the remainder of the event.

Glancing at her watch again, she realizes she has a few minutes before she needs to be in her seat. Deciding that another soda would be a good idea for a quick caffeine boost, she retrieves one. The sweet liquid is a lifesaver and will do the trick. Returning to her assigned position at the table, she checks her watch and is pleased to see she has three minutes to spare. Her primary goal at work and in her personal life is to be punctual in all her endeavors. Dependability is paramount in all her activities. Although this is her training, she strives to apply it to her everyday life.

***

As a limousine driver, you often have a lot of downtime while waiting for your passenger to return. During events like these, drivers typically spend the time between drop-off and pick-up, chatting and sharing stories. They all know the code of not sharing personal or sensitive information about their passengers; most conversations revolve around cars, traffic, and travel routes.

However, the other drivers do not take long to question Bobby about his passenger today. He is not surprised, as she is hard to ignore. The other nine drivers all noticed the petite blonde in her black-and-white outfit leave his car to enter the building, her smile and confident walk evident. They have many questions: Who is she? How was she included? And why is she dressed so differently?

Bobby shrugs his shoulders. "No comment, guys. You know the rules."

Shortly after their initial questioning, the event center door opens, and as if on cue, Number Ten steps outside. His heart sinks for just a moment, thinking she might not have made the cut. However, she stands outside for a few moments before turning to head back inside. With a brief wave, she re-enters the building.

Again, the drivers begin to question him, speaking all at once.

"Alright Simmons, spill!"

"Come on man, don't make us beg."

"Tell us who she is."

"She's definitely different from the guy I brought to this event."

"What's her story?"

Once again, the curious drivers urge Bobby for more information about his unusual passenger. Bobby shakes his head and refuses to divulge anything. The drivers respect his loyalty but continue playfully bombarding him with questions.

Bobby, smiling, locks his lips and throws away the key. They all enjoy this antic, and laughter ensues.

***

Reluctantly, the team agrees with Marcus to make a significant cut immediately. Before Rodney announces the cut, they ask Maggie to inform the drivers to return to their cars and prepare for their respective passengers, who might be affected by the cut. The group retains numbers 3, 7, and 10 for the exercise.

The same male voice comes over the intercom sixty minutes after the first announcement.

"I would like to thank you all for attending today's blind interview event. We know this was a short-notice event, so your dedication to the job is appreciated and not unnoticed. Our team and the potential employer have reviewed all your documents. Decisions are difficult. That said, if you are not chosen today, it doesn't mean you are unqualified; it simply means you may not be the best fit for this employer's current circumstances. Please remember that we recognize the talent and education in this room."

He pauses before continuing, "You were all assigned numbers for today's event. I will now call out random numbers. If you hear your number, please exit the building and return to your arrival car waiting for you. Our drivers are prepared to take you to your preferred destination. Once again, thank you for attending today, and we wish you all well."

Beth holds her breath as the announcer calls out the random numbers: 9, 1, 2, 4, 6.

She feels a moment of compassion as she watches the five eliminated interviewees exit the room, leaving behind the hope of securing a high-profile position.

The male voice begins to speak again after the five have exited the room. This time, his voice sounds more hesitant, announcing that an additional two candidates will also be cut: 5 and 8.

***

Following Maggie's instructions, all the drivers return to their limos and take their positions behind the wheel, preparing for the exit rides.

Soon after, they watch as five candidates begin exiting the building and returning to their assigned cars. From the blank looks on their faces, it is clear they are disappointed not to have made the first cut.

When five interviewees exit the building and no one else follows, Bobby exhales, realizing he had been holding his breath. He had been praying not to see Beth leave. Just then, the door opens again, and the sixth candidate emerges, followed by the seventh, but thankfully, still no Beth.

The remaining drivers look at each other, somewhat confused. Bobby is also momentarily puzzled; normally, only half of the candidates are cut in the first round. He muses to himself, "Of course Marcus is cutting them all right out of the gate."

Then, he smiles, realizing Beth has not exited; she seems to have made the first cut. He looks around the parking lot and sees two other limousines remaining.

***

Beth, unaware she was holding her breath while waiting to hear her number, lets out a deep sigh. Her number was not called. Until now, she hadn't realized how much she wanted to prevail in the first elimination. As she glances around the nearly empty room, she notices that even the receptionist has left. She guesses her part in today's event is over. The room, which felt quiet before due to everyone's silence, now seems even larger and more still. She is certain that the weight of uncertainty hangs heavily in the air.

Beth briefly allows herself to feel excited about making the first cut, knowing she still must complete the exercise portion. She smiles internally, knowing the security piece will be her strongest asset in the interview. She is great at appearing stoic on the outside, so it seems she keeps her composure externally. The three remaining interviewees sit and patiently wait for further instructions; each says good luck to the others.

The remaining three watch intently as a door at the back of the room opens; Rodney Wilson enters and strolls to where the three candidates are sitting. He is a well-dressed, fifty-something-year-old man. His walk is confident as he approaches them, and his smile looks sincere. His attitude is both professional and friendly. He greets each of the remaining applicants by their last name only. He congratulates them for advancing after the first cut and tells them about the next session.

He explains they will be performing a security detail exercise. The potential employer and his team will be reviewing the exercise live as they complete it. He then requests that the three candidates follow him to the door through which he just entered. Without hesitation, the small group rises and does as asked. The adjoining room is smaller than the one they spent the morning in. This room is cozier, with a couch, some chairs, and a table with coffee and sweets. Tucked away in the corner, there is a larger table. Beth can see and recognize from across the room that the table holds a variety of weapons: guns, knives, tasers, and stun guns. Upon closer inspection, Beth realizes they are not real weapons but props. Rodney encourages the candidates to choose any weapon or combination of weapons they might incorporate into their security detail.

He provides them with an outline of the remaining event following the completion of the security exercise. He states that each interviewee will have a brief one-on-one question-and-answer interview. He will ask each candidate to answer a series of questions, informing the trio that this portion will be in front of their peers; it is not a private Q&A. After completing this process, the next portion of the session will allow the candidates to ask him individual questions, again in a group setting with their peers.

Lastly, he informs them that it is time to begin and let the process unfold. Each candidate will perform the exercise in numerical order: first, number three, then number seven, and finally, number ten.

Marcus and his team watch in anticipation as the three prospective applicants prepare for the exercise. As they choose their arsenal, Marcus is slightly surprised by their weapon choices. Numbers three and seven choose traditional weapons, while number ten chooses entirely different and unpredictable weapons.

"This should be interesting," Marcus mumbles, still not convinced she is security detail material due to her petite size. Mancuso continues to sit quietly, smiling, knowing that each is White's perfected weapon of choice. He also knows firsthand that she is very proficient with them all. He may have taught her how to use them, but she perfected her skill. He waits patiently for the show he knows she is about to put on for Marcus.

After a few moments, Rodney notifies number three that they are ready for the interviewee to compete in the exercise. Waiting is the hard part. Within an hour, number three has returned, beaming with pride. Beth knows this means he thinks he has aced the exercise. Rodney once again enters the room to notify number seven it is time to compete in the exercise. Just as number three, he also emerges within the hour with a look of satisfied pleasure on his face. By their appearances, Beth gathers they have completed the exercise well, without a hitch. Both three and seven are men, not that it matters to her.

Marcus appreciates the talent of the first two candidates. He agrees with his team; they were both poised and professional, but he still doesn't feel a personal connection to either of them, even though he is trying. For the bodyguard position, both would be excellent, but he needs a personal assistant, someone around him every day. The security aspect of the job is a bonus; after all, he already has two of the best bodyguards on his team. He doesn't only want to feel a connection with whoever he hires to fill the personal assistant position; he needs to. Whoever he hires will be spending a lot of time in his personal life. He must have someone with a great personality who thinks like him.

Rodney returns for the third time; it is number ten's turn to complete the exercise. Beth has chosen a small stun gun, a .22

pistol, and a small dagger for her weapons. The stun gun is a 10,000-volt pen light. It has a clip, fitting perfectly into Beth's pant pocket. She places the .22 handgun into a holster on her waistband, slightly in front of her left hip. Due to her last-minute outfit change, she has to improvise the small dagger's location. Usually, she straps it to her ankle; however, due to her last-minute outfit change, she chooses her left upper arm instead. Beth is instantly thankful that she packed the tank top worn underneath her oversized shirt, as she unbuttons another button.

Each time Beth puts on her weapons, she immediately goes into a state of high alert, transforming her entire persona. She becomes invincible, sometimes to the point she is unrecognizable, even to herself. Beth is not oblivious to the positive and negative comments others have made about her during her career. She lets neither affect her ego. Not being conceited, Beth knows she is well-trained and can hold her own, and then some.

Due to her petite size, people often underestimate her abilities. Today, she feels reasonably sure that the other two candidates in the room do not consider her an obstacle for the same reason.

Now it is her turn to compete in the exercise, time for her to showcase her talent.

Trying to remain positive, Marcus has little hope of being impressed by her. He imagines that her petite size will reveal her flaws during the exercise. He glances toward Mancuso but is unable to read his expression. His attention returns to number ten, waiting to see a weakness.

He watches intently as the exercise begins. Beth is met by Rodney, Maggie, and a dog when she enters the next room. She receives her exercise instructions based on the scenario of what she will protect. The man and the woman are walking the dog. They will encounter various situations that require Beth to react and defend. The exercise goes off without a hitch. Beth protects the couple as expected. The woman, the man, and the dog all make it safely to the end of the exercise.

Marcus watches her closely as she pets the dog. She speaks to Maggie and asks Rodney, "How is your day going?" All are genuine interactions. Then, he watches intently as B. White maneuvers the pair and the dog to safety whenever she detects the need to do so. She doesn't overreact to the planned, non-threatening situations. Yet, when needed, she takes down an actual threat with minimal effort, using her arsenal efficiently. With Beth's reaction times and precision, Rodney seems genuinely impressed, if not surprised.

When the exercise is complete, Marcus is both shocked and pleasantly surprised, clapping his hands in excitement. He wonders if he might have just found his new assistant. Mancuso, still sitting quietly, smiles as he watches Marcus's reaction to the outstanding show she has given them.

Choosing not to be transparent, unlike the other two candidates, Beth is nonchalant when she joins the others back in the waiting room. They all sit quietly, waiting for the next phase. It is apparent that each of them is replaying and reviewing their exercise performance over in their minds, wondering if their actions showcased their talents to their fullest potential.

A few minutes later, Rodney joins the remaining three in the waiting room. He starts by asking each candidate two individual questions. Most of the individual questions are as expected and generally generic to the job. He then follows up with a couple of questions asked to the group before focusing on the questions asked of him by the interviewees. The question-and-answer portion is routine, and again, Marcus is impressed with number ten's knowledge and understanding. She is both well-educated and well-spoken. Marcus now knows her CV is on point, legitimate, and not fraudulent as he had initially suspected.

Although Marcus is sure about who he feels a connection to for the position, he understands that it's only fair to review and discuss all three interviewees as a team.

Marcus and his team decide to send the group home for the night, with the final selection to be made the next day.

* * *

Rodney returns to the waiting room and thanks the interviewees for their patience, applauding their performances. He informs the three candidates that the process has concluded, and that the potential employer will review each folder and video documentation from the day. He advises them that one of the three applicants will be contacted within twenty-four hours for a face-to-face meeting with the potential employer. At that time, an impromptu interview will take place and a discussion of a possible contract will occur. He commends them on their talent, wishing them all good luck as he instructs them to exit the building.

Three hours after the initial cut, the final three candidates emerge from the event center. As they exit the building, they exchange well wishes and handshakes before heading toward their designated cars and drivers.

CHAPTER SEVEN

Bobby exits the limo as Beth approaches. He planned to open the back door for Beth to enter the backseat, but when he saw her grimace, he smiled, immediately opening the front passenger door, as he chuckled.

"I know, you've got shotgun."

As Beth collapses into the comfy seat, she is overcome with an instant calm relaxation. The excitement and tension of the last five hours begins to dissipate as the softness of the cushion cradles her. She lets out a deep sigh, proud of herself for taking this unplanned adventure, no matter what the outcome.

Five hours. Wow, who knew any interview process could be so lengthy? She considers herself savvy in her security field but had no idea such events existed for interviews. She is grateful for this experience Mancuso has provided for her.

As Beth gets comfortable in her shotgun position, she flashes Bobby a kind smile and asks jokingly if he missed her while she was gone.

Bobby responds with a nod and a slight chuckle. Yes, he was curious, but he doesn't want to pry. Instead, he starts the car and proceeds back towards the city. After a few minutes, Beth speaks.

"So, you're not even going to ask me how it went?" "I figured if you wanted me to know, you would share without any prompting from me, but since you brought it up, how are you feeling about the day, the whole process?"

"Truthfully, the entire day was interesting. I never knew such a thing existed, and I'm happy to have gotten the experience. Mancuso said this was a once-in-a-lifetime chance, and he was correct. I still think the concept is a bit strange, but I understand its reasoning. I'm pleased with myself for taking this last-minute opportunity. I came and showcased my talent; I did my best. That is all I can ask for."

Even she was surprised to admit she enjoyed every minute of it, as odd as the interview seemed initially.

She continues providing Bobby with a brief recap of the exercise.
"I enjoyed the exercise; everything went off without a hitch. The man, woman, and dog are all safe, which is always the main goal. Getting an 'all clear' is the best reward to receive."

She was pleased with her performance and felt she had done well. Beth knew she performed her best when working with others in her field, even if it meant competing for a job.

"I enjoy being in my zone, doing what I love, protecting others."

By her tone, Bobby knew her words were true; she was the real deal. Bobby didn't say anything aloud, but he could relate to what she said and knew the exact feeling she was describing.

***

Back at the Event Center, lengthy discussions were occurring concerning the pros and cons of the day. Marcus and his team reviewed each other's comments, concerns, likes and dislikes. Ultimately, a decision was agreed upon; it was unanimous. B. White was the standout of the day, hands down.

Marcus can hardly contain himself. He surprises everyone when he excitedly convinces Rodney to call Bobby, asking him to bring number ten back to meet him tonight. Marcus doesn't want to wait until tomorrow; he needs to meet her in person tonight. He can't wait to meet this woman face-to-face. He is eager to extend her a job offer and have her on board as part of his team, as soon as possible.

Traffic is light, and Bobby and Beth continue talking back and forth as he navigates the limo towards her hotel. After only a few short minutes on the road, Bobby excuses himself from their conversation, saying he needs to take an incoming call on his earpiece. Bobby is surprised to hear Rodney's voice; even more so when he asks Bobby to return Beth to the event center.

"Bobby, the boss is requesting to meet your passenger tonight. I know we said tomorrow, but he wants to offer her the job tonight."

Surprised, Bobby answers simply,
"Yes sir."

With the call disconnected, Bobby looks at Beth and sees the concerned look on her face. She had not heard any of the exchange, only Bobby's short, vague response. She is almost afraid to ask, but she has to know, "Is everything okay?"

Bobby had only met this extraordinary woman this morning. He is both shocked and excited to inform her they were requesting Beth return to the event center. She has been chosen for the position, and now she was meeting the boss tonight.
"That call was Rodney requesting that I return you to the interview center."

Beth was not entirely clear on what he was saying. She doesn't know what this means. Have they made the cut already? She needs him to tell her exactly what is happening. Keeping her tone even, she asks quietly, "So Bobby, what does this mean?"

"Hold that thought. There is an empty parking lot ahead; I will pull into it. Then we can talk, and I will give you all the details."

Once he brought the car to a halt, he turns to face Beth. In a low, even tone, what he said next took them both by surprise, "You are their pick. You got the job; it is time for you to meet the boss. Tonight."

Beth took a deep breath; they picked her. This was really happening. What a day!

"Now? Tonight? I thought they said tomorrow."

Not listening for him to confirm her questions, her mind flashed back to twenty-four hours ago, when she was sitting in her pajamas in North Carolina. Suddenly, she burst out into laughter. Bobby watched her intently, afraid she was having a breakdown of some sort, possibly delirium due to lack of sleep.

"Don't be alarmed, Bobby. I am only recalling the expressions on everyone's faces when I entered the room this morning. I didn't fit the mold; I was the unlikely candidate. Normally I, too, would have been dressed exactly like them, in a gray suit and expensive shoes, only not carrying a briefcase. Except you were early, and I had to dress in my Plan B outfit. Now the boss wants to meet me."

Bobby's smile relaxed, recalling how he had also thought she was the unlikely candidate when he first met her this morning at the airport. Beth's following words were not expected.

"Before we return, I have one simple request: will you stop at the nearest gas station and get me some caffeine and candy? In case you are unaware, I have been awake for at least thirty-six hours. I must be alert if it's time to meet the boss."

This time it was Bobby who burst into laughter when he realized what she was saying.

"Are you telling me you just aced a high-profile interview, including a security detail exercise, and you are sleep-deprived?"

Beth had not given it much thought as she nodded, then she joined him in laughter.

"Imagine how awesome I am when I am rested. Otherwise, if the boss can provide lots of caffeine and candy, I can operate for days."

She giggled as she continued with lighthearted conversation, recalling her busy day and non-traditional interview attire. Bobby obliged her request and stopped at a gas station for her caffeine fix. Then they were once again on the road, heading back to the office building they had just left.

Bobby could only imagine how tired she must be, even though she didn't appear it, she was still pleasant and smiling. He even considered calling Rodney back and asking if they could wait until tomorrow. He was impressed with her and wondered how she had not crashed, but he also knew firsthand the coping mechanisms taught in training. She stated she had been awake for over thirty-six hours; this was just another example of her strength and determination; one he would make certain Marcus knew all about.

***

When they arrived back at the Event Center, Bobby drove to the enclosed private parking garage in the back of the building, not stopping in the front lot as before. When they approached the locked gate, he promptly entered the code to open it. The now-open enclosed garage revealed a small parking area with two cars and another limo.

Beth's mind was racing as she instantly thought Bobby must have been here before. She had not realized, however, that she had spoken the words out loud until she heard Bobby respond.

"Yeah, I have been here a few times."

Then, he was silent, not elaborating any further.

Bobby had many things he wanted to say to Beth before meeting with Marcus, but there was so much he couldn't share. Instead, he guides Beth from the limo towards a door marked as a private entrance. Before opening the door, Bobby pauses, and Beth thought she heard him say, almost in a whisper, something like "permission to mute." He knew he should not break his professional confidence, but he wanted Beth to succeed. So, he made a split-second choice, one he hoped he wouldn't regret.

"Remember our conversation from this morning? It's the same thing tonight, okay? Be confident but be you."

Beth nodded, confused by Bobby's strange behavior. Before she could question it, he said, "Good luck in there, Beth."

In an instant, he reached out and pulled her into an embrace. It was a brief hug, but it was long enough for him to whisper in her ear.

"Beth, the boss is a famous guy. Stay strong and keep focused. Do not falter; stay calm."

"Don't be a fangirl; you've got this."

Surprised, and caught off guard, Beth nodded as Bobby let her go abruptly. Turning back toward the door, he quickly swipes his badge, silently hoping Beth understands what he said to her. In one swift motion, the door was open, and Bobby is ushering Beth inside. Now he's guiding her down a hallway to what she assumes is the boss's office. It was a different office than the one before, but it shared a similar feeling, warm and welcoming. This office appeared more business-oriented but still inviting. Two men were waiting for her as she entered.

Rodney, a familiar face, greets her with a warm smile and a handshake, thanking her for her prompt return.

"I know you have had a long day; thank you for returning. I promise it won't be much longer."

He then introduces her to the other man in the room, telling her his name, Donald Hare. Donald shakes her hand and tells her he is the financial consultant for his client. Beth exchanges pleasantries with both men, still curious about the employer.

She takes the seat as offered and waits for the meeting to begin. After she is seated, Rodney turns his attention to Bobby, asking him to join them. Confused, Beth is not sure what her limo driver has to do with her job assignment. Bobby took a seat in the back of the room, out of the way, as Rodney requested. Beth had little time to process much of the situation before Rodney begins explaining and reviewing the day's events.

Rodney and Donald both praise her natural ease, skill, and talent in stressful situations.

In the back of the room, Bobby sits quietly, intently watching as Rodney and Donald recapped today's events. He was sure Marcus had made the best decision, as he was truly impressed by watching this woman's calm and professional demeanor. Beth nodded modestly and thanked them for their praise and comments about her performance. More importantly, she thanks them for the opportunity to attend today's event and the possibility of future employment.

***

Marcus and Mancuso are waiting patiently on the other side of the door. From experience, he finds it is better to let Rodney and Donald "break the ice" about his identity whenever he is meeting someone new. They describe the position, give a brief overview, and then reveal his name moments before he enters the room. By doing it this way, it helps to lessen the shock and awe when Marcus joins them. Their excitement never bothers him, and truthfully, he still doesn't get all the hype he creates. However, it is what it is, so he finds letting them drop his name before he enters makes it easier to communicate with them, giving them time to be somewhat coherent enough to have a conversation.

Now the moment arrives for Rodney to reveal the name of the high-profile person she has been interviewing for all day. She prepares herself to meet this secret, famous employer. However, she felt the goosebumps form on the back of her neck, when he proudly announces that the potential employer is world-renowned mega rock star Marcus Donovan. Of all the names she was prepared to hear, this was not one of the top one hundred. Just hearing his name and the thought of working for 'him' actually rattles her. Just the sound of his name shakes her to the core. This was huge, she was not expecting someone of his magnitude. This thunderbolt revelation leaves Beth momentarily stunned.

The instant jolt of shock was immediately followed by a surge of admiration. Beth knew the potential employer was someone important, but it's Marcus Donovan. She recalls Bobby's strange actions and words before entering the building. Now she understands. She wonders if he has known all along who the interview was for.

She hopes her unmistakable reaction wasn't unprofessionally evident, or if they did, she recovered quickly enough for Rodney or Donald to barely notice. As if on cue, all eyes in the room were on her. Everyone is watching and waiting anxiously to see her reaction after they disclosed Marcus's name. Maintaining her composure, Beth meets them with a warm smile. Outwardly, her smile never falters. She is trying her hardest not to "fangirl" as Bobby had instructed.

CHAPTER EIGHT

Regaining her poise, she tries to appear nonchalant, remaining calm. Still processing the revelation of what she just heard, the office door opens, and Marcus Donovan and his security guard, Mancuso, walk in. When Marcus enters the room, all eyes in the room shift back exclusively to Beth.

Even with her strong willpower, her reaction to his entrance is a little more evident than she wished to show. However, it was brief, with only a small gasp as her breath caught in her throat. He is such an icon, a name known worldwide, and here he is standing right in front of her, even more attractive in person than one could have imagined.

Her legs and hands tremble only slightly as she stands to introduce herself, reaching out for Marcus's hand. She hopes all this is barely noticeable as she manages to recover quickly.

Marcus notices the brief tremble in her legs as she stands, as well as the slight shake in her hand as she greets him with an extended hand for a handshake. Instead, he unexpectedly takes her hand and places a small kiss on the back of it, and he can't help but notice her eyes are wide and friendly. "It is a pleasure to meet you finally, Beth."

Mancuso was not wrong; this woman is special. She is warm and kind, and you can feel her energy just by being in the same room as her. He felt it in her hand, small and warm.

Beth's voice is strong and confident, yet she is not sure how, as she thanks Marcus for the opportunity to attend today's event. She knew she probably shouldn't, but she couldn't help herself when she added that she is a huge fan. The latter statement seemed to please him, and his response to her is accompanied by a bright smile.

"So, we both appreciate each other's work. I would say it sounds like we are off to a great start."

Beth met his brilliant smile, noticing how it shone in his eyes as well, trying desperately not to gush over the man standing before her.

Marcus takes charge and motions for everyone to have a seat. Once everyone is seated, Marcus leads the discussion of the highlights from the event, especially those making Beth stand out.

Interestingly, they all make sure to comment on their amusement at everyone's reaction as number ten entered the room, also adding they knew when she walked into the room, she was the one to watch. Beth knew exactly what they were referring to and not being able to hold back her words she responded with a light tone.

"Yes, because I had on my Plan B outfit."

Bobby, who was sitting quietly in the background, doesn't hold back and breaks out in laughter. The room was temporarily confused and the sound of his pure and genuine laughter triggers Beth to join in. Puzzled as to what was funny Mancuso also joins the laughter. He knows she is talking about today's outfit. What she wore today is not her typical, professional attire. He isn't sure what the story is, but he knows it will be a good one, and he cannot wait to hear all the details.

Rodney, Donald, and Marcus are also not aware of what's so funny about her clothing, but they still smile at the sweet sounds of the rooms laughter after such a long day.

Laughter felt good, setting a lighter tone to the atmosphere. After a few moments, it had quieted down and Bobby was the first to apologize for his outburst. After several more minutes of business talk, Marcus asks everyone to give him and Beth the room so he can privately discuss the opportunity with her. He watches his team leave the room and giving instructions for Bobby to wait at the limo. He nods to his boss as he closes the door quietly, leaving the room.

After leaving the office, Bobby heads back to the limo, waiting for further instructions. He mulls over the events of this unscheduled day. He is grateful he agreed to meet Beth at the airport, and he has been a part of today's journey with such an extraordinary woman.

***

When everyone had left the room, Marcus asks Beth to join him by sitting in the chair next to him. She is still mesmerized to be talking to Marcus Donovan; she is not sure if she can trust her legs, but she does as he requests. He smiles and jumps straight to the reason they are here. His next words sound genuine and sincere.

"Beth White, I will be honored to have you as a member of my staff. But one other thing before we proceed, do you have your cell phone with you? I want us both to record the next part of our conversation."

She nods, as they both retrieve their phones for recording purposes.

"Great. We will both open our cameras and record our conversation about my employment proposal. The reason I want an electronic record is for both of us. I do not want to miss any of your questions, and I want you to have verbal documentation of my answers."

He is also concerned that it is the weekend, and with his rehearsal schedule, she could change her mind since contracts would not be finalized for a few days. Honestly, Marcus doesn't want to wait until Monday, mostly for himself, also he wants her to feel secure in his job offer. Employment contracts are not generally in his wheelhouse for new employees; he has never jumped right into this portion of the hiring process, but he can't take a chance on losing her by putting her off for even one day. Marcus wants her to know he is serious about her joining his team, sooner rather than later. He wants, needs, her on his team.

He needs to secure a digital recording of her agreement to the position once she knows the terms. He can't risk losing her. Marcus focuses on strictly discussing business matters once both cameras were recording and lying on the table before them.

"Beth, if I am being perfectly honest, I am not entirely sure of your exact duties. I guess we can learn together; this is a new position for me. So, this means we will make it up as we go. If that is OK with you."

She smiles at his honesty, and a small chuckle escapes. Looking at Marcus, she notices the sheepish, boy like smile on his face watching her intently.

"Beth, don't worry, I am guessing the position is straightforward. Now the next part, I feel secure, and again, if it is not correct, we will revisit the topic at the 'real' contract signing."

"Again, this dual security/personal assistant position is new territory to me; I believe the salary is in the 150K range. If this is incorrect or not enough, we will revisit the amount. I am unsure which documents Rodney and Donald will need you to complete, but I wanted you to have as many details about the position as possible, before you accept or decline. If you agree to my employment offer, my legal team will have the necessary contracts ready for you to sign on Monday."

Lastly, he informs her of his intention to help out by providing local housing for her, since she would be his assistant. He requests that she be local and available, possibly daily, as he needs her. As the topic is being discussed, Marcus makes another generous offer. Hoping to make today easier for her, he offers her a room at his estate in the wing designated for staff until housing can be arranged. Beth agrees to this invitation. She can't imagine how beautiful the Donovan mansion must be.

"Mr. Donovan, the position sounds amazing. Thank you for the opportunity. I am honored you chose me, and I am pleased to accept your employment proposal. I look forward to our new venture together."

"Beth you earned the position; it is me that is honored."

The video-recorded meeting now concludes, and he places a call to the mansion arranging for her to have a room in the service quarters. He asks his housekeeper to prepare a small snack and turn down the bed in the pink room. Before ending the call, he turns to ask Beth if she has any special requests. Still bewildered by the day's events, she says, "No."

Marcus is pleased with the meeting's outcome as he welcomes Beth to his team. When they both rise, hands are shaken to seal their arrangement. He returns his focus to his phone, texting Bobby, requesting for him to return in order to escort Beth back to the limo, stating she would be returning to the mansion with them tonight. Within minutes, Bobby is back in the office as requested.

Beth is impressed with how disciplined, yet comfortable everyone is around Marcus Donovan.

"Bobby, I need to brief Donald and Rodney before we leave. It's about the important information we need to add to Beth's contract. I should be able to wrap it up quickly and meet you at the limo. It shouldn't take long, I estimate it will be twenty minutes or less."

Beth leaves the office with Bobby; her mind is reeling from this unexpected day. They are both silent, her exhaustion is catching up to her. She feels it deep to her core. What an unbelievable day this has been. She is in awe; she just landed a job with Marcus Donovan. Did today just happen to her? Was this real, or is this a sleep-deprived delusion?

With all the excitement and the rush of emotions, she could feel the caffeine fix was long gone, and she couldn't wait to sit and process all the day's events.

As they approach the limo, Bobby states matter-of-factly, "Sorry Beth, you are in the backseat tonight. No more shotgun."

They both laugh as Bobby opens the door. He settles Beth into the backseat, leaving her alone with her thoughts, as he's sure she is overwhelmed with her long day.

Beth climbs into the vast backseat; she's amazed at how huge it was. Her only experience inside a limo was one that was much simpler and smaller than this one. The limo is dark inside, with low ambient lighting. Music is playing softly over the speakers, Marcus's music, of course.

Beth instantly feels her entire body begin to shut down, she is sleepy for the first time since boarding the red-eye last night. She relaxes, entirely at ease, leans back, and closes her eyes. Her intention is only to let her mind revel in the day's events. However, she unintentionally dozes off not long after she attempts to replay them in her head.

Marcus had told Bobby he would join them after the brief meeting, which he estimated would take no more than twenty minutes. He checks his watch as Mancuso is escorting him to the limo. The meeting had taken him fourteen minutes to update his team and finalize his hiring instructions for Beth. He found himself hoping that Beth would find his promptness impressive, showing her he makes every effort to keep his word. When they arrive at the limo and the door is held open for Marcus to enter, he vaguely catches the silhouette of Beth's petite form. Both men realize she has fallen asleep when she doesn't turn towards them at the opening of the door. When Mancuso takes his seat beside her in the limo, before Marcus could protest, he attempts to wake her.

Slightly awakened, Beth becomes vaguely aware of Mancuso sitting beside her. Still not alert, she also briefly notices Marcus is sitting on the other side of her. Beth stirs, compelling herself to wake up.

She is so sleepy, unable to keep her eyes open; they are so heavy. If only she could have a couple more minutes, just a couple more. This is Beth's last memorable thought as she nestles her head on Marcus's shoulder and drifts back into her slumber. Marcus finds he doesn't mind this gesture at all. He is surprisingly relaxed as this tiny warrior finds a peaceful sleep, using him as her pillow. Her even breath sounds are mesmerizing, and Marcus cannot remember the last time he felt so comfortable. His only thought is, only nine hours ago, she was B. White, number 10, an unimaginable CV to consider, a stranger. Now, she is Beth, a member of his team, asleep on his shoulder, and he could not be happier. He knows now at this moment; he made the perfect choice.

Bobby is watching the rearview mirror as Marcus enters the limo. He sees when Marcus recognizes that Beth is exhausted. He doesn't seem to mind and is now allowing her to sleep soundly on his shoulder, although she didn't give him a choice. He cannot help but notice Marcus seems very comfortable and relaxed, allowing his shoulder to provide a safe place for her head. During the entire ride to the mansion, Bobby keeps glancing in the rearview mirror and can't help but smile. He smiles, thinking we all need a number ten in our world.

CHAPTER NINE

Beth awoke in an unfamiliar bed with no immediate knowledge of her surroundings or how she had gotten here. It took her a few minutes to focus, and she suddenly recalled the events from the previous day. She notices that she is still fully dressed, wearing the clothes she wore to the interview, her Plan B attire. She saw her shoes were placed neatly beside the bed. Scanning the room for her luggage, she spotted it on a stand in the corner.

She looks at her watch, and is momentarily shocked to see the time was 8:00 A.M. She experienced a brief moment of confusion before remembering she was in Las Vegas and no longer on the East Coast. This time change will take some time to get used to. Still, she mused, 8:00 A.M. was later than she usually slept. She silently decides to give herself some grace as she went so long with no sleep.

She sat up and surveyed the room, forcing her mind to recall the previous day's events that had led her here. She shook her head, speaking only to herself.

"You don't have time for this, young lady; you'd better get moving; the day is almost gone. Whoops, my bad. Only chickens are up at this hour on the west coast."

Her pep talk made her laugh, as it sounded like something her parents would have said to her when she was younger. She hopped off the bed, making her way to the adjoining bathroom. She was instantly impressed by the massive space. Upon entering into the room, she catches her reflection in the vanity mirror, almost not recognizing the image staring back at her. She was shocked when she saw her head of unruly, tousled hair. She let out a small laugh.

"Oh my! What a sight you are Beth."

"Shower," she said aloud when she spied the large walk-in shower.
"I need a hot shower."

She walked over and turned the water on. While waiting for the water to warm, she returned to the bedroom to retrieve clean clothing from her luggage. She desperately wanted to get out of this outfit; not only had she put it on twenty-four hours ago, but now she had also slept in it.

Back in the bedroom, she opens her suitcase. As she is grabbing her necessities, along with a much-needed change of clothes, she allowed a laugh to escape her lips as she again remembered the details of the previous day and how surreal it all was. She would have thought it was all a dream, a wonderful one, if she weren't standing in the middle of this massive room, which she was sure was in a mansion. Her mind quickly flashed, thinking, what do you wear in a mansion? A mansion owned by Marcus Donovan, at that. She chose an outfit that fell between casual and formal. She smirked as her eyes landed on a familiar piece of clothing, she stared at her gray suit, her business attire, then she quickly tossed it out of the suitcase, stating matter-of-factly,

"So much for your help yesterday. I did it without you."

With clothes and necessities in hand, she made her way back to the walk-in shower. Only then did she fully pay close attention to its large size. Now that she had gotten into it, she estimated it was almost as big as her entire bathroom at home. Thankful for the many jets, she utilized them to stimulate her skin. She hoped they would help alleviate the lingering jet lag she felt.

As she allowed the hot water to soothe her, her mind wandered to Marcus Donovan. He was not as tall as she had imagined, maybe five-eleven. His frame was medium but also slim; she was sure plenty of muscle was hidden beneath his clothing. His features were astonishing in person; she was certain photographers loved him, now knowing firsthand they did not photoshop any of his pictures. Oh, but his smile and his eyes told the real story of him as a human. She mentally noted to herself that he was the most handsome man she had ever seen in person. She surmised and finally admitted he was definitely the perfect male specimen

Now showered and dressed, she instantly recalls Marcus telling her to wait for him in the limo to continue their conversation. Suddenly, panic arose in her chest, and it felt like a golf ball was in her throat. She must have fallen asleep before he joined her, and now she was panicking.

How had she allowed that to happen? She has never behaved so unprofessionally in her career. She has trained to be stronger than this. By her standards, sleep deprivation was never an excuse, regardless of the circumstances. She must talk to Mr. Donovan immediately. She needs to make him understand that this was a one-off, an isolated incident, and not normal behavior on her part.

She quickly made herself presentable while repeatedly rehearsing how she was going to apologize for her unprofessional behavior. The bottom line was simple: she was embarrassed.

Not sure where she was going, she exited the bedroom and proceeded down a beautiful staircase. The bottom of the stairs opened into a vast living area. Scanning around the room, she noticed a small table tucked away in the corner. She notices that the table had coffee, fruit, and other breakfast items. She was making her way toward the table, when Mancuso entered the room.

"Well good morning White. I didn't expect you to be up this early"

"Hey Mancuso. Yeah, my body thinks I'm still on east coast time. I just was on my way to get a cup of coffee to clear the cobwebs."

She was trying to sound matter-of-fact, praying she had disguised her embarrassment.

Knowing her well, something felt off with her and Mancuso immediately called her out on her unusual tone and behavior.

"Are you OK?"

When she turned to face him, his smile faded as he saw no smile on her usually smiling face. What he saw was remorse, perhaps a hint of failure, which confused him. "What's wrong White? Has something happened?"

"I messed up Sarge. I need to see Mr. Donovan. He said he wanted to talk to me when he got to the limo last night. Can you believe that I fell asleep before his return? Oh my gosh, what have I done? A good agent never falls asleep."

Mancuso breathed a sigh of relief that her crisis was nothing more serious than her falling asleep. However, he also knew her thought process, knowing she was very strict when it came to the job. She was her own worst critic. Choosing his next words carefully, not wanting to dismiss her feelings but also not encouraging them, he said,

"White, Marcus is not in the least bit upset. He knows that you had a very long day. He really is a very caring and thoughtful man."

Beth knew Mancuso would always be straight and to the point with her. She trusted him fully because of it. Still, it took her a few minutes for these few words to sink in, and a few more to allow herself some grace in the situation. She needed to try to accept that Marcus did not see her as a failure. She looked to Mancuso, who nodded, making her realize Marcus understood. Beth still felt uneasy about any negative impression she might have created. Choosing to believe Mancuso and what he was telling her; she silently vowed that this was a one-time instance and would never happen again. She took a deep breath and sat down with her coffee.

"So, let's talk about why you didn't give me a heads-up about 'who' this once-in-a-lifetime event was for when you invited me."

"White, you know I would have if I could. Confidential standards and all."

She knew this would be his answer before he gave it, and she understood and accepted his explanation of anonymity.

She was sure she knew Mancuso better than anyone else, even though they had not seen each other for years. He was her trainer when she started security services. However, he became more than a mentor as he and his wife took her and Mark in as friends when they were stationed away from home.

She was with him the day he got the shocking news that changed his life forever: the unexpected accident that took his wife and child. Mancuso was a strong man, but this incident affected him beyond everyone's expectations. He took leave and disappeared for a month to grieve. Upon his return, he was more solemn than usual; work became his mistress. Before long, he was totally immersed in perfecting the job and became completely consumed with it.

As she sat here recalling their history, she wondered how much of Mancuso's history he had shared with his current friends and employer. Her thoughts were interrupted when she realized Mancuso was talking to her. She turned her attention back to what he was saying.

He was telling her that Marcus had left instructions for the staff to allow her to recharge and reset today. He needed her to know he was aware of the exhausting day she had yesterday. Marcus wanted her to know he apologized for calling her back last night instead of waiting until today as planned.

"Marcus is requesting to meet with you when he returns from the studio this afternoon."

This surprised her, hearing he was already awake and gone.

"Wait. He is already at the studio? Does he always get up and out so early? Of course, I will be looking forward to meeting with him when he returns."

"Yeah, he is not much of a morning person, so I am glad Bobby is with him today. Anyway, he tries to get out and back in before Vegas wakes up fully and realizes he is away from the mansion."

Mancuso was smirking as he tried to hide a small laugh.

"You wouldn't believe what this man has to go through on the daily. But he is a good guy. I am happy he saw your potential. I am glad to be working with you again White."

"Ditto my friend, Ditto."

They both then settled down to a bold cup of coffee and chatted for a few more minutes.

"OK White, I have got to get to work. Boss has a meeting scheduled; I can't be late."

She nodded and said, "Thanks again for giving me this opportunity. I won't let you down."

"The thought never crossed my mind. Welcome to team Donovan."

"Thanks again. See you later Sarge, I think I will go outside for a bit to clear my head."

"That's a great idea White; the pool is a nice oasis; you will find a visit there very relaxing."

Now alone, she took a sharp breath of relief allowing herself to find a peaceful calm. The last forty-eight hours were hectic; she was ready to let her mind unwind. Mancuso's idea about a visit to the pool was brilliant. She now felt the overwhelming urge to get out into the sunshine, where she could breathe, knowing it was exactly where she needed to go to clear her head. Nothing was more refreshing than when she could feel the sun's rays warming her skin, allowing her to feel refreshed.

Additionally, she recognized her desire for the need of a quiet space, she needed to process yesterday's events and reflect on how she had arrived at her current destination. Again, her mind whirled, and the memories came full circle. Her emotions were a mixture of excitement and even a bit overwhelming. She shook her head, still in disbelief. Was this her new life? It was true. Here she was in Las Vegas. She was at Marcus Donovan's mansion; his newest employee, that was where she was.

CHAPTER TEN

She easily found her way outside; in awe of the breathtaking and beautiful landscape in front of her. Aside from the Las Vegas Strip, she knew very little about Nevada; however, she was certain gardens such as these were not typically found in the desert. Come to think of it, she did not even know exactly where she was right now and made a mental note to ask Mancuso when he returned from his meeting.

Without much effort, she located the welcoming sight of an oversized pool surrounded by chairs and brightly colored umbrellas. It was a warm and happy vision, so vivid and perfect that it didn't look real, but rather like a picture from a magazine. She reached a partially shaded chaise nestled under one of the colored umbrellas. She relaxed and closed her eyes as she stretched out, feeling the warm, dry air of the morning sun on her body.

Only when she was fully relaxed did she allow herself to reflect on all the previous events that had brought her here today. Recalling them made her smile, beginning with her phone call from Mancuso, her impromptu flight across the US, and wearing non-traditional interview attire. The event, and then meeting Marcus Donovan, only to be offered the job as his assistant.

She had been waiting for an opportunity to begin a new chapter in her life, and it looked like Las Vegas would be the starting point, at least for a while.

She felt calm as she tried to anticipate what it would be like working for Marcus Donovan. Surprisingly, she was not anxious at all; instead, she felt at ease and comfortable, which she had not felt in a long time.

She smiled as she reminded herself of how the entire day had unfolded yesterday; it was real, it had really happened, and she was not dreaming.

She remembered the magazine she had grabbed from a small table in her room, picking it up she mindlessly leafed through the pages, not focusing on any images. Once again her mind began to wander about nothing specific, yet about everything. She sat back and closed her eyes, feeling the warm, dry heat on her legs.

She must have drifted off, as she was awakened by hearing someone softly call her name. The sweet tone was beckoning her awake.

Beth opened her eyes; she was stunned to find herself staring directly at Marcus's face, directly into his hazel eyes.

"Oh my, I have done it again, haven't I?."

She quickly sat upright. Her heart leapt as she tried to contain her embarrassment; she was sure her face was red; maybe Marcus would think it was the heat.

Her first reaction was anger towards herself for her vulnerability and for appearing weak, as once again, he had found her asleep. She immediately worried about how he perceived her. What did he think? Although she could do the job, did she appear lazy and seem to require a lot of sleep? She was genuinely concerned about how Marcus viewed the situation, viewed her.

"I assure you Mr. Donovan, it is not normal for me to fall asleep anytime I get still."

She hoped she had kept her tone even and that he did not sense her embarrassment in her apology.

Marcus was smiling, almost chuckling.

"All humans need to rest; believe it or not, even I sleep. It should be me apologizing for making you endure such a long day."

Beth took a deep sigh of relief. She could tell by his concern and kind eyes that he meant exactly what he said.

"Yet some little birdie told me you were up and out at daybreak today."

Instantly she wondered if she should have said anything, she was only trying to change the subject and lighten the embarrassment she felt.

"I'm sorry. I shouldn't have said anything. It's just I went to talk with you earlier and was told you were already up and gone."

He shrugged his shoulders.

"Yeah, now that you are an employee, you know my big secret. But I will let you know another one that you will find amusing; I am not a morning person."

"So, I also heard about that too, Mancuso filled me in."

"Good to hear your little birdie revealed my secrets."

She saw his boyish grin and knew she hadn't crossed any imaginary lines

He hesitated for only a brief moment before beginning to speak again.

"Anyway, I hate to intrude on your well-deserved relaxation, but if it's okay, I need to talk with you about something important."

Beth saw concern and worry on his face, fearing he was going to say he had made a mistake yesterday. Was Marcus already having concerns about hiring her? Then again, maybe he only wanted to talk about whatever he had planned last night.

She was now concerned this adventure might be over before it had even begun; was he already second-guessing his choice? Second-guessing her? Her mind raced as she tried to devise a plan to allow her to walk away voluntarily. It would be a much lesser blow to her ego and self-esteem; after all, she had not yet started working for him. She was afraid to say much, as she was sure her voice would quiver, but she gathered her dignity and began,

"Mr. Donovan, if you would like to dissolve the verbal agreement we made last night, please be assured that I will delete my voice recording right now in front of you."

Beth saw a kind and reassuring smile spread across his hazel eyes as he quickly began to clarify the confusion he sensed in her voice.

Running his hand through his hair, he never expected his hesitation to appear this way.

"Oh no, no, it's nothing like that. You are perfect for the position, and I have no regrets. Not last night and not today."

"We are going to make an excellent team. Of this, I am sure. It is something else entirely. A project I have been planning and working on for a while. I just learned this morning that all the pieces have come together, and it will happen sooner than anticipated."

She was surprised at his response, and she was even more surprised by her own wave of relief. Less than forty-eight hours ago, in her downtime, she had no plans for the next few months. Now, she had landed a position as Marcus Donovan's assistant. Thankfully, she managed to sound matter-of-fact, yet interested, without being too curious when she met his eyes.

"I am intrigued. If you feel inclined, I would love for you to share this recent development."

Marcus took a deep breath, thinking about how to spring such a life-changing idea on someone he had just met twenty-four hours ago. He also knew this had to be in total confidence, so he needed to remind her that Donovan Inc. now employed her before he could reveal his plan.

"Remember, as my employee, there's always full confidentiality between our conversations."

She nodded in acceptance, thinking she had learned this early in her career. In her profession, confidentiality was her number one priority; she then quickly remembered that Marcus did not know her, so he was being cautious.

Searching for the right words, Marcus wasn't sure where to start or what to say. Well, he knew what to say, just not how to say it without sounding like a crazy, paranoid person. He decided it was best to blurt out the short version, leaving it open for her to ask questions and initiate a follow-up conversation.

"I am leaving Las Vegas tomorrow."

Her thoughts immediately jumped back to her first intuition: the job was over. She sucked in her breath, feeling like she had just been sucker-punched.

Marcus recognized her confused and hurt expression and quickly shook his head to let her know she had misunderstood his statement. He wanted, needed, to give her all the information before she could refuse.

"The plan is for you to accompany me if you agree. I'll fill you in on all the details once we're on the plane, if that's okay. It is a long story."

She noticed the mixture of concern and sadness in his eyes. Yet she wasn't sure why announcing that they would be travelling was such a big deal; she traveled worldwide with her clients.

She also did not understand why leaving tomorrow on short notice was such a big deal. She surmised that with celebrities, you never know what they think is important. Perhaps he felt that since they hadn't completed all the contract paperwork, she might have a problem leaving with him.

"If it is the paperwork you are concerned about, I really have no worries. I trust you to keep your word, Mr. Donovan. We have the recording. That is enough for me, for now."

"It's not the paperwork but thank you for your trust in me. Anyway, I had the contract drawn up this morning. We can review and sign it tomorrow on the plane if that's okay with you. That is, if you still agree to the position."

"That sounds like an excellent plan, and I look forward to our travels tomorrow."

He was pleasantly surprised by her quick agreement to this unusual situation. As he rose to leave, he paused and asked her a final question.

"Is there any family you need to inform about your travel, as we will probably be off the radar for a while?"

"No, just me. Not even a goldfish at home to miss me." She tried to sound carefree as she forced a smile with her response. Marcus noticed her slight sadness but decided the timing was not right to ask yet.

Her heart was breaking, as she wished there was someone to inform. Her mind automatically shifted to Mark and how much she missed him. She was sure he was her guardian angel, and he was always keeping a watchful eye over her.

As she watched Marcus Donovan's tall, slim figure stride away, she recalled how Mark was always so proud of her work, she was sure that he would also be excited about this new position. She glanced towards the heavens and whispered,

"Miss you babe; watch over me during my travels in this newest adventure."

CHAPTER ELEVEN

When the heat became too much, Beth decided it was a good time to explore. She spent the remainder of the day enjoying the beauty of the mansion and met many of the staff members. Her biggest surprise was discovering that a mansion this size could feel warm and welcoming. Even with the many employees hustling and bustling around, it felt comfortable, like a home should.

Still wanting to relax, the heat of the day forced her to remain indoors. She decided to try again to read the bestseller she had begun forty-eight hours ago. She found a small vacant room with a cozy chair and lost herself in the book's pages.

The chef briefly interrupted Beth with a small plate of fruit, sweetly inquiring if she wanted anything else. Then, she proceeded to inform her of the dinner schedule to ensure the food would be to her liking. Beth assured her she was not complicated and that anything would be fine with her. Momentarily, she was confused by all the fuss to please her, as she was also an employee. She finally accepted that they were all just being friendly and trying to help her feel welcome in her new environment.

***

After leaving Beth at the pool, Marcus returned to his office, where he found Bobby and Mancuso impatiently waiting. Before he even reached his chair to sit down, Bobby blurted out the question they all wanted to know. "So, what did Beth say?"

Before Marcus could respond, Bobby noticed a look of despair on Marcus's face.

"You didn't tell her the whole story, did you?"

Marcus shook his head in dismay. How was he supposed to tell someone he just hired that he was leaving and not returning? The media was destroying him. For his own sanity, he must find his way back to himself. He was tired of the constant circus surrounding him.

"No, I didn't tell her everything; I promise I will. Beth agreed we can have a full discussion on the plane before the contract is signed. She told me that she trusted me, and I still didn't disclose everything. I feel terrible. I will make it clear she has no obligation to stay with me. I suppose I'm selfish; I like her. I think we will work well together."

Tony Mancuso, normally the strong, silent type, recognized Marcus's distress. He spoke in low tones but with reassuring authority.

"White will understand, boss. Don't be so hard on yourself. She might be shocked when she first hears all the details, but she never shies away from an adventure. It's not as if she must stay in isolation with you forever. She will always have the freedom to leave whenever she desires."

The three men then began discussing the getaway plan, the outline, and the timetable for the next day.

Months ago, what had initially started as an imaginary "what if" conversation had somehow taken on real life. The idea was, "what if" Marcus could leave the limelight and quietly disappear for a while?

The more the men discussed the possibility of making it a reality, the more they realized they might really be able to pull it off. Soon, they began laying the groundwork, with Marcus setting up two separate, untraceable bank accounts: one for Mancuso, another for Bobby, both containing a large amount of money.

Bobby purchased a 50-acre ranch in Oklahoma, located in a remote area, far from the nearest tiny town. Bobby and Chloe were excited about relocating and calling Oklahoma their permanent home. Ranch life enticed them all. Bobby and Chloe would move into the recently updated and spacious house. They decided for Marcus to have a home built with his own custom design. The home intended for Marcus was still in the early stages of planning, and both men were excited for

Marcus to begin in his new surroundings once the plans were finalized and construction was complete.

Mancuso used his account to purchase an isolated, private island, accessible only by helicopter or boat. He had purchased both. Recently construction had been completed, which included a mini-mansion and a security house. Top notch security was installed with the latest and greatest, by far the best to date.

Marcus had yet to visit either location but was excited to do so. Truthfully, he was even more excited at the thought of relaxing and enjoying time outdoors at both locations without the fear of paparazzi lurking around every corner.

Marcus's island getaway was now ready for occupancy. Staff and security team were already in place, with only one holdback: waiting for the final piece, the boat's arrival.

Today. Today was the day. Mancuso was notified this morning of the boat's delivery to the docks. Everything was happening quickly than anticipated, as they thought it would still be months before it all came together. Delivery of the boat, the first adventure in isolation had become a reality. Marcus, anxious for a break, didn't want to waste time relocating to his new residence, thus prompting his quick travel plans.

Marcus called it 'tired,' while others called it 'burnt out.' Marcus called his getaway freedom; he only wished to be free to enjoy his life without being continually under the industry's microscope. The media was ruining his life, which hurt him tremendously. He loved performing and his loyal fans, but sadly, he needed to walk away for a while; he couldn't do it anymore. He felt he had lost his enjoyment, his spark. He had lost himself to the world.

CHAPTER TWELVE

The morning sun dared to glisten in the east when Marcus, Bobby, and Beth arrive at a small private airport the following day. Mancuso is already there, waiting outside the jet. Beth isn't sure who she expected to be traveling with them, but she is pleasantly surprised to be greeted by Mancuso's familiar smile. She's also surprised when her gaze falls on Bobby climbing the steps into the jet behind Marcus. The chauffeur seemed to be perfectly content to be included; Beth leaned in and ask Mancuso in a whisper.

"I wasn't aware Bobby was coming."

"Of course, he is Marcus's best friend, he's family."

Shortly after they have taken their seats, they are airborne. Within what feels like only mere minutes, the pilot announces it is safe to move about the cabin.

Marcus wastes no time and invites everyone to join him at a small table near the rear of the cabin. Again, Beth notices Bobby is included, and she makes a mental note to ask Mancuso more about him later.

As they all take their seats at the table, Beth notices Marcus appears nervous as he pulls a folder from his briefcase. He seems hesitant and pauses before handing Beth her employment contract.

"Before you review the contract, I need to discuss something with you, Beth, full disclosure."

"Sure, Mr., um, I mean Marcus."

Marcus shoots nervous glances between Bobby and Mancuso, taking a moment to gather his courage, then he begins to tell Beth the truth about this trip.

"Beth, you must understand that fame is suffocating the life out of me. I need to get away from the public eye to breathe freely again. Almost a year ago, a discussion among friends about an imaginary getaway took on a life of its own. I now own an island and a ranch, thanks to Bobby and Tony. The ranch is still in the early stages, but the island is complete and ready for me to take occupancy.

I'm excited about enjoying a life of freedom without the world watching my every move. I can't promise what your job duties will look like, but I would still love for you to join me. We never expected everything to come together so soon. Honestly, I can't wait another minute to enjoy my solitude."

She listens intently, suddenly feeling sorrow knowing this man's only answer for peace was to escape to an unknown location.

She chooses her words carefully, unsure how he expects her to respond.

"So, it seems you've given this a lot of thought and gone to great lengths to arrange something special. We'll make sure you get the rest and privacy you deserve."

She has many more questions, but they can wait. She picks up her employment folder.

"Now, let's review this boring paperwork part and get the contract signing complete and out of the way. It sounds like we have a new adventure ahead of us, as well as an island to explore. Let's go find some peace and quiet for you."

All three men let out a deep sigh, relieved she is agreeing to be part of Marcus's plan. Truthfully, they are comforted knowing Beth will be with Marcus.

As she reviews the contract, she finds it exactly as they agreed. With no issues, Beth signs every page, and Marcus shakes her hand, formally welcoming her to the team.

"Thank you for staying on the team. Please know you are free to leave whenever you want; you are not obligated to stay isolated and locked into my craziness."

Beth nods and excuses herself to return to her seat, claiming she wants to get back to the novel she can't seem to finish. However, when she tries, she can't focus on the words, replaying the plan of isolation she has just been presented. Now, Beth realizes how the chauffeur fits into the picture. There is more to the story, but the pieces are beginning to fall into place.

Marcus has a team helping him go off the grid, which is interesting. It seems he has no intention of returning to his world of fame. What will this look like? Will he still be writing and recording? She tries to imagine how hard it must be to be an international personality with no privacy. It makes her sad to think his musical career might be over. Even sadder is the thought of how bad things must be for him to consider this his only option. She is heartbroken for Marcus, thinking of the extreme measures he is willing to go through just to have some peace and quiet.

Her thoughts shift to her role, wondering what an assistant does for someone in seclusion. Beth is almost certain her security skills won't be needed. She had been excited, hoping this would be an unforgettable adventure traveling the world with a rock star. Marcus's final words were to assure Beth she wasn't locked in and could break her employment contract at any time if the seclusion didn't suit her.

Even though she thought the job would be more, the idea of seclusion sounds good for an entirely different reason. She has nothing waiting for her at home but sad memories, but she refuses to let them interfere with what is happening here and now. Truthfully, her one main concern about this adventure is how long it will be before someone finds him.

***

With not a clue as to where they are , the jet lands at the private airport. Mancuso's voice gives everyone comfort as he begins to take charge automatically.

"In case you're wondering how we will get to the docks; I also bought you an SUV. I feel we have less chance of a paper trail than if we rent a car. Today we'll use it to travel to the docks. I've secured a parking spot there for our future use. Today, we'll travel to the island by boat; the helicopter hasn't arrived yet. Hopefully, it will be here in the next couple of months."

Beth can't help but be amused, thinking this is not a conversation you hear every day, discussions about helicopter deliveries.

Bobby is efficient and wastes no time loading the luggage into the back of the SUV before giving Marcus the all-clear to exit the plane. A faithful chauffeur, he ensures all passengers are settled comfortably for the drive to the docks.

Bobby settles behind the wheel and Mancuso sits in the front with him. Beth thought she heard Bobby say something about shotgun, but she didn't question him. When they arrive at the docks, Beth is shocked to see a large public marina. She is relieved when Bobby navigates to an isolated area away from the other boats. Beth marvels at how well Bobby and Mancuso protect Marcus from unwanted recognition.

Marcus's excitement is evident as he sees the shiny red boat tied to the dock, this is his boat. He is like a child, anxious to explore. It's not huge but larger than average. Even with its size, it doesn't stand out or scream, "My owner is somebody famous." Beth notices the words painted on the side of the vibrant red vessel: *New Beginnings.*

Marcus also notices and turns to Mancuso, giving him a thumbs up.

"New Beginnings. I love it!"

"I was hoping that you wouldn't mind the name. Very fitting don't you think?"

"Yes indeed. It is perfect"

As the small group boards the boat they are greeted by the captain, Frank, whom Mancuso has employed to provide transportation to and from the island. Frank is a weathered, elderly gentleman who probably isn't aware of who Marcus

Donovan is; or maybe he is, and it doesn't matter to him. He informs them that the trip to the island will take about forty-five minutes.

Being a gentleman, Marcus asks Beth,

"I'm sorry, I didn't think to ask you beforehand, will you be okay with an extended boat ride, or do you need to sit down somewhere?"

"Thanks for asking Marcus. I'll be fine. I've never experienced motion sickness, so yep, I'm good, I have sea legs."

Marcus smiles and nods to Captain Frank.

"Great, then I suppose we're ready to go."

With Mancuso by his side, Marcus begins exploring every inch of his new vessel shortly after leaving the dock. Beth hears him say repeatedly,

"This is perfect. You made an excellent choice, Tony."

She smiles at the childlike joy in his voice. She's also not accustomed to hearing anyone call Mancuso by his first name except for his late wife, yet Marcus has done it several times.

They navigate smoothly through the water, barely feeling the waves as the boat cuts through them effortlessly. Beth stands silently, watching the horizon disappear as they travel out to sea. She realizes she still has no idea where they are. She assumes they must still be in the U.S., probably off the coast of Florida, since they didn't go through customs. The weather is beautiful, and she makes another mental note to ask later, her list is getting long.

Still gazing at the ocean, lost in thought, she sees a tiny island coming into view.

"This must be the place."

Beth thinks she is alone until she hears a voice beside her.

"Yes it is. This is Marcus's new home."

She recognizes the serious tone and turns to meet Mancuso's gaze.

"White, I hope you understand my situation. Don't be mad at me for being so secretive. When I added your name to the interviews, we had no idea Marcus would be moving to the island so soon. This is some last-minute adventure I got you involved in."

"I'm not mad, and of course I believe you Mancuso. Truthfully though, it really is a lot to take in at once. I have so many questions, I don't even know where I am."

"White, you know I trust you explicitly. I would have shared it all if I could have, but you know I'm bound by contract. Marcus has become a trusted friend, as I am to him, but he's still my employer. I'm glad you trusted me enough to take that red-eye flight from NC. I hope you remember I always have your six."

Beth knew Mancuso would always have her back, as she would have his. With an acknowledging pat on his arm, she assures him she understands.

"I don't ever need to be reassured. I know you do, and I hope you know I'll always have your six as well. However, a little backstory would have been helpful…kidding. We both know if I were in your shoes, I'd have done the same thing. The job is the job, period."

Mancuso accepts her response with a playful elbow nudge.

He knows she's right.

"White, Marcus had no idea this whole seclusion plan would happen this quickly; you must believe me. Truthfully, I'm almost certain I would have tried to hint to you about it if I had known."

She believes him. They stand silently, trusting in each other as they approach the island.

CHAPTER THIRTEEN

Mancuso and Bobby gather their belongings while Marcus, ever the gentleman, steps off the boat in front of Beth to assist her onto the dock. The gesture was sweet, and she must admit she has missed a man assisting her every once in a while.

Captain Frank announces he will stay anchored for two hours before returning to the mainland. He confirms that Bobby will be the only passenger returning this afternoon. Bobby nods.
"No problem Captain, I'll be here."

Bobby and Mancuso have created alternating schedules. They will alternate, each spending one month at a time on the island. Since it was Mancuso's responsibility to set up the location, it made sense for him to stay first to familiarize Marcus with everything.

The small group takes their first steps towards Marcus's secret getaway, down the newly built dock. Behind them, anchored securely, they leave the shiny boat which says it all, New Beginnings. Walking toward the brilliant white sand, they marvel at the beauty surrounding them. Beth asks aloud,

"This beach is amazing. What is the name of this beautiful paradise?"

Mancuso shrugs, giving Marcus a quick pat on the back.

"That's a job for Marcus. He needs to name his kingdom."

All eyes turn to Marcus. Hearing the exchange, he knows he'll choose the perfect name later. For now, he is speechless, in awe of its beauty.

"I will have to find a name that's fitting for this paradise."

Once they have stepped off the dock, they continue toward two parked golf carts. Marcus, however, stops, removes his shoes, and takes a deep breath making a joyful declaration. "Home Sweet Home."

He wiggles his toes in the warm sand, smiling. Beth watches his features relax, enjoying this simple gesture.

"The only time I've ever walked on the beach, with the sand beneath my feet, was when I first arrived in California. I've wanted to do it again, but I never had the chance. I will now be able to do it every day. I **will** do it every day."

Bobby and Mancuso smile and exchange fist bumps. Pleased already, they can see Marcus relaxing. Lately, he has seemed "off," and they are relieved to see this familiar version of him return.

However, Beth isn't smiling. She feels sadness for him, thinking how hard it must be to be world-famous yet unable to do simple things like walk on the beach. It strikes her as unfair that he must give up his life and the things he loves to do because of fame. Prior to today, she has never given much thought to the life of a mega rock star. Now she realizes it isn't all the glitz and glamour she has seen Sammie enjoying.

The golf cart ride to the house is short. From the boat, the island looked tiny, and now she wonders about its true size, another mental note to add to her list.

Within a few short minutes, a break in the trees reveals what at first glance appears to be a quaint, not-so-little house. The closer they get, the more she sees it's actually a two-story mini mansion.

"This is beautifully amazing. I'm bewildered to think it has recently been constructed specifically for Marcus."

Mancuso proudly announces,

"Welcome to the Triple M."

He explains the name means "Marcus's Mini Mansion."

Marcus loves it and can't stop smiling.

"I love it Tony! This is perfect, my new life, my new beginning."

Thinking of the boat and the Triple M, he momentarily gets overwhelmed with emotion. He is thankful for Mancuso, who always knows what he needs, even before he does. Today confirms what he already knew: even if he weren't famous or his employer, Tony would still be a great friend.

As they approach the steps, a woman with a bright smile opens the door. She introduces herself as Rosie, the housekeeper.

Marcus isn't surprised by her appearance; he knew Mancuso had hired staff, including a housekeeper and a chef. Staff schedules are already set. They will arrive weekly on Wednesday mornings and leave the same night. Once a month, they will stay overnight and leave Thursday at lunch, but they are flexible. It's only a forty-five-minute boat ride, and *New Beginnings* can make the trip easily. Soon, a helicopter will be available for quicker transport.

Marcus and his team follow Rosie inside the massive door. The all enveloping warmth that greets them makes Marcus sigh in relief. Once inside, Mancuso instructs Rosie to show Beth to her room on the ground floor, reminding her that Beth is her "go-to" person if she has questions or issues.

Beth smiles as Rosie leads her to her new bedroom. Rosie tries not to seem anxious, but it is obvious she is, as she has never met anyone famous. As she assists Beth into settling in, she relaxes, realizing Beth is not demanding, in fact, she seems a bit embarrassed to be waited on. Rosie finds Beth's smile kind and feels a rush of excitement at the thought of working closely with her.

"Ms. Beth, please let me know if you need anything. No request is too large or too small."

"Thank you Rosie. Please call me Beth, I am an employee just like you. I too, am also new to this whole celebrity thing. I look forward to working with you. I am here if you have any questions about Mister…."

Her voice trails off, unsure of what she is allowed to disclose.

"It's OK Beth. I know he is Mr. Donovan. His secret is safe with me."

***

With Bobby in tow, Mancuso starts the grand tour of Marcus's new home.

"Tony, I know we discussed every detail during construction, but I cannot express the love and warmth I feel right now. My heart feels instantly at home, and it has since I first walked in the door. You have truly outdone yourself, my friend."

"I am glad you approve boss. I have a lot of things to show you."

Mancuso's first stop on the tour is Marcus's office and studio; both located on the ground floor. Neither are extravagant, but they are perfect. Briefly at a loss for words, Marcus is amazed that the rooms hold all the equipment he could possibly need. Next they head upstairs to the massive master suite, the only room on the second floor.

As they enter the room, they are immediately drawn to the wall of windows showcasing a stunning view of the ocean. As if drawn by a magnetic force, Marcus continues walking until he is touching the window.

He shakes his head in awe, unable to find the words to express his appreciation for Mancuso's efforts. When Marcus brings his focus back to the room, he notices a large bed strategically placed to face the ocean, a piano tucked into one corner, and a chair with his guitar beside it. A small desk with a computer creates a mini office nearby.

Just when Marcus thinks he can no longer be surprised, he recognizes a deeply personal touch, something only those closest to him would understand. They know he likes having the ability to play and document new ideas for music and lyrics whenever inspiration strikes, whether while sleeping, resting, or even in the shower.

Bobby is also observing the room's setup, but his focus remains mostly on Marcus. He recognizes the raw emotion on his friend's face. Sensing that Marcus is speechless, he pats him on the back.

"Looks like you're all set with this new life boss man. Mancuso has thought of everything. Time to relax and give us your next platinum record. A song named Bobby sounds like a good place to start."

Marcus looks at his friend, silently thankful for the comment that broke the silence.

Mancuso witnesses the exchange of unspoken gratitude and understands Marcus's appreciation without needing words.

"Oh my! Now he wants a song named after him! Okay, now let's continue with the tour while Bobby is still here. We can't let Captain Frank leave him with us one minute longer than needed. Next thing you know he will want to name the island Bobby."

They laugh as Mancuso continues jokingly, "I guess you don't need a tour of the bathroom; you know what those look like, right?"

"Unless you've added something unusual, I think I can explore that alone."

With the tension of unspoken thanks gone, the three friends laugh as they head back downstairs, listening as Mancuso describes the new home's amenities while briefly visiting each room. Bobby can be heard making up lyrics about an island named Bobby.

"Do you mind crazy man? I need to finish this tour and see you off this island."

"I might just stay and help Marcus write a song."

"No! Anyway, Marcus I'm sure you're curious about security. It's in a separate location, not within the house. It is out back, a standalone Security House. Follow me."

They follow Mancuso through the large kitchen and out the back door. Less than three hundred feet away stands the Security House.

Mancuso has hired a small elite team, Jackson and John, to monitor the island's security around the clock. Either Mancuso or Bobby will also always be on the premises.

Marcus is unsure what to expect as they enter, but the sight before him is impressive. The room is filled with monitors and high-tech equipment. For a moment, he wonders if this might be overkill, considering they are in the middle of the ocean. Then he recalls the many instances when people breached his personal space. Paparazzi would do anything to capture a shot or get a story. This memory reminds him why such extensive security is necessary.

Marcus greets both men casually, thanking them and assuring them that their talents are greatly appreciated. He tells them he is always available should they have questions or concerns. His sincere smile surprises them, and they are relieved to find him friendly and approachable. They appreciate his offer but know their direct contacts will always be Mancuso and Bobby.

Feeling more at ease, Jackson and John eagerly show Marcus the scrambling shield that protects the entire island, preventing cyber breaches and drone activity. They give him a watch with instructions on how to contact them at any time by pressing a button.

They explain that only three people have the authority to activate or deactivate the cameras and protective shield: Marcus, Mancuso, and Bobby.

Marcus is left speechless, recognizing the lengths his team has gone to protect him. They know his needs even better than he does. He is humbled to have them in his life. What started as a "what if" conversation has turned into reality because of Mancuso and Bobby's dedication.

Before he can dwell on his gratitude, Mancuso leads the tour to the living quarters for Jackson and John. Then they adjourn to view two, slightly larger, additional rooms designated for Bobby and Mancuso. Bobby notices Mancuso's luggage already placed in one of the rooms.

"What! You got to pick the best room? I think this one would be perfect for me. I should've known you'd pick the best one."

"Quit being such a whiner dude; they're the same size."

Playfully shaking his head, he looks at Marcus. "Are you sure this was the best you could do when you paired me with him?"

"Sorry guys, I'm a bit limited in the friend pool these days, so I guess you're stuck with each other."

Still laughing and teasing, they move on to tour the spacious common areas; the living room and kitchen, both warm and inviting.

Jackson and John have chosen to rotate their time on the island weekly, while Bobby and Mancuso will do monthly rotations. Marcus agrees this schedule sounds perfect.

Checking his watch, Mancuso notes that time is running short and Bobby still has to depart back to the mainland.

"Come hell or high water, we must get Bobby on that boat."

"You bet I'll be on that boat! I've already seen you show off way too much for one day."

They grab water bottles from the kitchen and head off on a golf cart to explore more of the island.

Not far from the Triple M, they reach a small but beautiful beach. Walking on the sand, Marcus finally finds the words he needs to say to his dear friend.

"Tony, I am thrilled with everything you've done for me. For someone who writes down their feelings for a living, I find myself at a total loss for words. So, I'll just say a heartfelt thank you man."

"I'm glad you approve boss. Honestly, I too am impressed and even a little overwhelmed by how it all came together.

Mancuso's voice carried both pride and relief, as he continued,

"Thank you for trusting me to protect and provide what you need in this new venture. I hope you find it's all you dreamed of and that you come home stronger than ever. However long it takes, we're here for you, always."

Marcus shifted, his words caught in his chest. Bobby senses he is struggling to find his words, he once again steps in to rescue him.

"Hey guys" he begins with a grin, "remember I've got something going on for the boss in Oklahoma too."

Mancuso glances at his watch, pretending annoyance, he doesn't miss a beat.

"Oh yeah, you're still here, huh? Don't you have a boat to catch or something?"

Their eyes meet, silently agreeing that their playful banter gives Marcus time to process his emotions.

"Yep, I'm still here. So, what else do you have? I need to see it all before I leave. I've got contractors waiting at the ranch, and I need to outdo you, though I will admit, you've set the bar pretty high friend."

"Good luck with that brother." Mancuso replies smoothly. "No way your ranch life will top my island life, but you can try."

"Oh, so now I see what you think of my abilities. Little ole me, the lowly chauffeur, and you, the big-time security guy who's been around high-profile stuff since before I was born. Excuse me."

They are all laughing, even Marcus has joined in. Marcus is amused because he also knows Bobby helped Mancuso with most of the planning of the islands details.

"Sorry Bobby, but Tony gets the gold star today. Maybe you can ask him for his contacts when you start building my ranch house. If only you had his connections."

With laughter still in the air, Marcus takes off running toward the ocean. Mancuso and Bobby look at each other, nod, and with a high five, say simultaneously, "Success."

CHAPTER FOURTEEN

Marcus and Beth are both grateful for the unexpected gift of this new, simple, and solitary life of sun and sand.

Beth is genuinely surprised at herself, as she never imagined she could find such satisfaction living a secluded life. In her wildest dreams, she never fathomed becoming an employee, let alone a friend and companion, of Marcus Donovan. Once their daily routine had been established, they instantly found a natural ease with each other. She is impressed by his structured schedule; even in paradise, he truly is a workaholic.

They meet at the breakfast table every morning. Some mornings Bobby or Mancuso join them. Beth is always amused by Bobby's quick wit and playful banter, while Mancuso, being more reserved, casually updates Marcus on the latest industry news.

Beth often catches herself smiling at the contrast between the two men. Somehow, on an isolated island, she has found stability and harmony.

Morning coffee and pleasant small talk set the tone for the day, before adjourning to Marcus's office to discuss business. On most days, it is just Beth and Marcus. When it's only the two of them, the conversations are personal. Each day, they learn something new about each other.

She soon realizes, she was right, when she sensed at their first meeting; that behind the fame, Marcus is just a normal guy. He just happens to be extremely talented and sought after by the entire world and undeniably good-looking, though even that is starting to feel normal to her.

In only a few short weeks, their friendship begins to develop. She enjoys his company and often has to remind herself that she is his employee and they are not on vacation.

Several times during their meetings, Marcus asks for her professional input on business topics. Beth provides advice on business structure and finance, surprising even herself with how easily she answers. She silently thanks Mark, her late husband, for encouraging her to pursue her education. For a moment, she gets lost in memories of her love.

After easy days filled with work, sand, sun, and ocean, Beth warms the chef's prepared dinners for herself, Marcus, and occasionally Mancuso or Bobby. Dinner conversation is always light, with no work topics, just stories and laughter. This is when Beth learns the most about Marcus, especially if Bobby or Mancuso begin reminiscing.

As each day passes, Marcus becomes more relaxed. He begins every morning with his first step on the sand and remains in awe of what Mancuso created.

If he is being truthful, he does not miss any part of his crazy life, except for his parents. He misses them but he knows it's better for everyone if they stay out of the country far from him, at least for now.

His team may believe the island is only a short-term, temporary retreat, however Marcus can see himself staying here indefinitely. He set out on this self-healing journey with no timeline, and he sees none in sight, and that's perfectly okay with him.

If he finds new inspiration along the way, it's a bonus. His mind is clear and refreshed for the first time in years, and he feels the familiar tug of inner emotions demanding to be documented. He hears music in the air and is once again excited about creating. Without studio demands and pressure, he feels inspired to do what he loves, on his terms.

The weeks seamlessly flow into months, and both fully relax as they grow accustomed to their daily island routine.

The weekly arrival of the rotating security team and the weekly visits by the chef and housekeeper, Rosie, happen seamlessly. Rosie arrives early every Wednesday, cleans the mansion, does the laundry, and leaves by evening. The chef always prepares enough delicious meals for the entire week.

Beth is responsible for preparing them for her and Marcus, as well as do minimal housekeeping and laundry between their visits. With the routine now fully established, the weeks progress flawlessly.

The better part of every morning is spent working together in his office. Sometimes Marcus compiles ideas or creates melodies; other times, he may bounce ideas around or they talk and learn more about each other. However, usually most of their deep conversations happen at the evening dinner table.

Marcus is not surprised that he finds it easy to talk to Beth, even sharing his childhood stories, ones he has only ever shared with Bobby. Over time, Beth also begins to feel safe sharing parts of her past with Marcus. He seems genuinely interested in her as a person and makes her forget she is his employee.

After their morning office time, Marcus spends his afternoons outdoors, soaking in the sounds of nature and the ocean, sounds only he understands. Later, he returns to his studio, trying to duplicate the melodies he hears as he re-creates them on various instruments.

Beth can hear him singing or humming the raw tunes. She knows they are unfinished but beautiful, and the final result will be phenomenal. He truly is a musical genius.

When Marcus is alone, he often smiles thinking of Beth, and grateful that she took a chance by attending his interview event. He remembers doubting her CV, but now he knows everything was real and she is so much more. She is, without doubt, the smartest one in the room.

***

In the evenings after dinner, Marcus notices that Beth leaves for nightly walks. He assumes she goes to a secluded beach nearby. She returns shortly after sundown, looking refreshed.

When he asks, she explains that she started walking daily to stay healthy after learning about her parents' health issues. After her walk, she sits in the sand to watch the sunset, which she calls the most beautiful sight she has ever seen. Privately, she has nicknamed the beach *Sunset Beach*, though she hasn't told him this yet.

Marcus also enjoys the sunset each night from different spots on the island, though he has never visited her secret place.

One night, after dinner, he asks if he can accompany her. She smiles and nods, deciding to share the name she gave her private spot.

"I hope you don't mind, but I've kinda called the beach *Sunset Beach*. There are no other words to describe its beauty."

"*Sunset Beach* sounds like a lovely name. I can't wait to see it for myself."

"You don't have to call it that. I only thought it was fitting after the first night I saw it."

"If it's okay with you, I'll wait until after I see it, and we can decide together if the name sticks. Do you agree?"

"I think that sounds like an excellent idea. But I'm pretty sure you'll agree after your first visit. There are no other words to describe how breathtaking it is."

"Promise you won't be upset if I don't agree."

She knows he is joking.

"I'll be waiting for your agreement on the way back home tonight."

"Touche."

***

They walked together to Beth's private stretch of sand; a hidden haven she fondly called her *Sunset Beach*.

"Alright, Miss Sunset Watcher," Marcus teased. "Lead the way. Make sure I get the perfect spot to witness this spectacular display you've been promising."

Beth smiled as they reached her favorite place.

"Just wait. I promise it'll be worth it."

"I'm trusting you," he said, grinning. "I can't wait to see something so breathtaking it leaves me speechless."

On the water's edge, they settled into the sand in quiet anticipation. Before them, a massive sphere of glowing orange sank slowly into the horizon, the dusky sky deepening behind it. In moments, the brilliant sun was consumed by the calm, blue-green water. The world dimmed to darkness, and the moon began to rise, soft, silent, and serene taking its place as the new guardian of the sky.

Marcus could hardly speak. He had watched the sunsets every night since arriving on the island, but this one, this one was beyond anything he'd imagined. He understood now why Beth always came here. It wasn't just a sunset. It was a moment that silenced the world.

"I thought I'd seen beautiful sunsets before," he finally said, his voice low with wonder. "But that... that was beyond words. Thank you for sharing this with me."

He felt something settle in his soul, a quiet joy born from the simplicity of it all, the sand beneath his feet, the sound of the waves, and this shared silence.

"I think I've fallen in love with your *Sunset Beach*," he said softly. "From this night on, that's what I'll call it. Would you mind if I joined you again sometime?"

Feigning an exaggerated foreign accent, Beth replied, "Why of course my lord. Your presence is always welcome at *Sunset Beach*."

Her accent was awful, delightful and hilariously awful, making them both burst out laughing. Through her laughter, Beth tried to keep up the voice, which only made them laugh harder. Gasping for air, she giggled, "I'd better never try that again. I'm sure I just offended an entire culture somewhere."

"I'm sorry to say, but I agree," Marcus said, still laughing.

They were still chuckling as they rose from the sand and began their walk back to the Triple M.

***

The next morning, Marcus was brimming with ideas.

"Beth," he said, eyes bright, "what would you think about adding a couple of chaise lounges out at *Sunset Beach*?"

"I think that's a great idea," she said. "Just know, I might stay out even longer in the evenings if I get too comfortable."

"I was also thinking of a small cabinet to keep towels and beach things for impromptu swims. Maybe even a shower to rinse off."

"Wow… that all sounds amazing. Thank you for putting so much thought into it."

"This is your home too," Marcus said warmly. "I want you to have everything you need. And… thank you for letting me share your private place."

***

Beth's days continued to be filled with the comforting rhythm of Marcus working in his studio. She loved hearing him create, each day different from the last, each sound beautiful. She had always admired his music, but witnessing the raw process unfold in real time gave her a new level of awe. It felt surreal, almost sacred.

Every night, they return to *Sunset Beach*, watching the sun sink into the sea, always insisting that *this* sunset was better than the last. Sometimes, after the new additions were installed, they would slip into the water for a quiet swim before ending the night side by side on the chaises, talking softly as the moon climbed higher.

CHAPTER FIFTEEN

Three months have flown by. Neither Marcus nor Beth misses the real world, as they both now refer to it. Bobby and Mancuso keep them updated with the entertainment industry, rumors and other news. Marcus listens, but most of the time, he is disengaged from the topic of conversation. He trusts them to make any and all proper decisions on his behalf.

However, today Bobby brings personal news: Marcus's parents have contacted him, and they are worried about his whereabouts. He is happy with his current situation and is in no rush to return to his life of chaos in the spotlight. Relaxed and extremely pleased, he has written multiple songs and created the framework for many more. More than anything, he is happy to be free and to be himself, but he misses his parents and is upset to hear about their concern.

"So, what did you tell them Bobby?"

"Not much. Only that you were safe and I was staying in frequent contact with you. They asked if I could send a picture, but they understood when I told them it wasn't a great idea."

"Maybe we can. Let's check with Jackson to see if there's a way to take a picture without any embedded info. You can mail it to them from Las Vegas when you return."

"That's a great idea boss. I'm sure he can figure something out. We can take one at the security house, and in the event the photo is scrutinized, as we know it will be, there will be no way to identify any background."

"This is perfect! Go check with him now and update me on how we can give my mom her requested picture."

"On it boss."

With that, Bobby rushes from the room in search of much-needed information and assistance from Jackson.

Entering the security house, Bobby doesn't immediately see him sitting at the monitors. When he calls out, Jackson emerges from the bathroom with a panicked look on his face.

"I promise boss, I just walked away, but I had to go—bad."

Bobby isn't angry but decides to have some fun with the young lad.

"What have I told you about drinking a hundred gallons of water while you're working? Of course you'll have to keep running to the bathroom. Are you sure you're not diabetic?"

"I'm sorry boss. I try to limit my intake while working. It's just that I like water – a lot."

"That in itself is not normal. Who likes water boy? It rusts your pipes."

"I'll cut back. Give me a chance to prove it to you."

Noticing that Jackson is getting visibly upset, Bobby decides to let the ruse go.

"Calm down young man. I'm just yanking your chain. Keep doing what you're doing—you're a great employee."

Bobby sees the relief wash across his face when Jackson realizes he isn't in trouble for briefly leaving his station.

"The real reason I was looking for you is that I need you to do something for Marcus. Is there a way we can take his photo without all the digital information attached? His mom is requesting one, and even though we'll be careful, it will more than likely get leaked. Don't ask me 'how' but somehow it always does. Anyway, we will need to make sure it can't be tracked."

"Yes sir. Give me a little time and I'll have a perfect plan on how to get his mom an untraceable photo."

"I had no doubt we could count on you. Thanks. I'll take over watching the monitors while you figure it out."

"Thanks."

CHAPTER SIXTEEN

Beth appears satisfied with their secluded island life, so it surprises Marcus when she informs him she will be leaving the island for a couple of weeks to attend to personal business.

"Marcus, you made it clear I was free to leave the island whenever I wanted. I need to go home for a couple of weeks, if that's okay with you. I need to check on my house in North Carolina."

Confused, since she isn't elaborating further, he can only agree. He wants to ask more questions, but he doesn't want to intrude; besides, she owes him no explanations.

"Of course. You've always had the freedom to go. I hope I made that clear from the beginning."

"I know, and you did. I wish I could stay here forever, but it's just a visit. I'll be back. I need to finalize a few personal matters. Hopefully, it won't take long."

He knows he shouldn't, but he asks quickly before changing his mind.

"I don't mean to pry, but is everything okay? Is there anything you need from me—or how can I help?"

"Island life has given me time to contemplate my personal and financial business needs. I need to return home to address them. I've decided to sell my house and buy a condo or townhouse closer to the airport, which will be less maintenance if I continue to be away for long periods of time."

"Beth, I'm sorry. I know this is a hard decision for you. You told me briefly about your husband, Mark. Are you sure you're ready for this type of permanent closure?"

"Truthfully, no. I'm not sure if I'm ready to sever all ties with my former life, but being a homeowner when my job requires constant traveling doesn't make financial sense. I haven't made this decision lightly. Honestly, it breaks my heart but owning a house when I'm never there makes no sense."

She doesn't confide the other reason: the uncertainty of knowing what the future holds for her as Marcus's employee. If he chooses to stay on the island indefinitely, will he continue to need an assistant? Where does that leave her? He seems well-adjusted, and sometimes she feels like she's taking advantage of him. The job he hired her for no longer exists.

She instantly lets her mind flash to Mark and their lost dreams. Her heart aches with the familiar feeling she constantly fights, recalling happier times in North Carolina while choosing not to dwell on the outcome. She will always grieve Mark and their lost future. A wave of sadness washes over her, but she recognizes what she must do. She must let the past go.

Tonight's dinner is slightly tense, the mood heavy, as they discuss Beth's return to North Carolina. She shares a more in-depth explanation of her reason for returning home, assuring him that she'll return as soon as possible once she has settled her affairs.

"I should have paid more attention when we had our business. I've never prepared a home for listing; that was always Mark's area of expertise."

Her heart aches a little more when she says his name out loud. She tries to recover quickly so Marcus won't see her renewed sadness. But Marcus notices. He always notices her sadness when she talks about Mark. He reaches over, placing his hand on hers.

"Take as much time as you need. It's not like I'm going anywhere."

The comment makes them both laugh, easing the tension and sadness slightly.

"I'll get Mancuso to make the arrangements for you."

Beth's travel path consists of taking *New Beginnings* to the mainland, flying privately to a larger airport, and finally changing planes to a commercial flight home. Three months ago, Beth would have thought this type of zigzagging to cover her trail was unnecessary, but now she knows Marcus's safety relies entirely on this type of travel.

She arrives at the airport in North Carolina without incident. She feels a mix of anxiety and excitement about going home, unsure of how the next few weeks will unfold.

Her neighbors are an elderly couple, Mike and Carol. Living next door, they have agreed to take care of her house while she is away. She is grateful for their help, knowing that without them, she wouldn't be able to travel and still maintain a permanent residence.

All they know about her profession is that she works in private security. Her position and adventures sound exciting to them, and they always ask about her adventures. Beth is unable to share much but offers them small snippets of insight into her experiences. She plans to tell them of her intent to put the house on the market when she arrives home, before meeting with the realtor in a couple of days.

She drives the rental car directly to her house. Once there, she sits in the driveway as memories flood over her, and tears begin to fall. She isn't ready to go inside, so she continues to sit in the rental car, simply looking at her beautiful home, imagining a different future.

"Dammit, Mark! We were supposed to live happily ever after. Now our dream house is about to be sold, and I'm all alone in this big world, missing you. I'm trying to go on with life. I feel bad having a happy life without you. Your last words were that you would always be with me, guiding me through this process. I need you now more than ever."

As Beth sits alone in her grief, crying quietly, she notices a colorful butterfly fluttering outside her windshield. As she marvels at its grace and beauty, she quiets and takes a deep breath, knowing she is making the right decision. Butterflies are a sign of change. Instantly, a sense of peace comes over her. She knows in her heart that this is her sign from Mark, a sign that he understands and accepts her reasoning for selling.

"Thanks honey, for understanding why I must do this. House or no house, you'll forever be in my heart, never forgotten. I love you babe."

Still composing herself and accepting her plan to sell, she notices Mike and Carol returning home.

When she crosses the yard to meet them, they are both happy to see her and invite her in for a visit. She shares her intentions to sell and asks if they will agree to be the local contact for the realtor. They agree to act as Beth's proxy for potential buyers as well as make sure her home is presentable for viewing. Beth is thankful for their support and willingness to help with matters that must be handled by someone locally.

Mike and Carol make Beth promise to stay in touch. They ask about her current position, as they always do, and show concern for her safety. Beth assures them she is safe, reminding them she cannot share details, and they respect her privacy. The visit is emotional, and they all agree to stay in touch after the house is sold and no longer hers.

***

Beth meets with a realtor and quickly begins arranging movers and renting a storage unit for most of her belongings. At the realtor's suggestion, she leaves enough furniture to stage the rooms. Knowing this means she will have to return when the house sells, she agrees.

Within days, she finds the perfect condo, knowing it's a good investment if she decides to resell it later. Its location in a prime area, not far from the airport, is precisely what she needs: a two-bedroom, two-bathroom town home. She knows it could also serve as an excellent long-term option for her if her current job were to dissolve.

With her present employment, she isn't sure when she will return, so she only moves in enough furniture to be comfortable. This makes her think of Marcus. If she remains employed, she'll only be home for short periods of time. The thought saddens her. Planning for her future after her current assignment makes her feel an odd sense of loss. She scolds herself out loud.

"Come on Beth. This is just another job. You're getting too attached. This is your real world—your future is here, not there. Not even perfect positions last forever."

Even though her brain knows this is true, her heart still aches at the thought of the day she no longer works for Marcus. She would miss him. She likes him, a lot.

She tries to convince herself that it is only the seclusion she enjoys while on the island. Again, she makes a mental note not to get too attached to the island or Marcus.

Shaking her head as if to knock sense into herself, she says out loud,

"Stop! Get your head in the game and your heart out of it. You must operate with your head for success. Missing a position or job means you're getting too involved. This is not how Mancuso trained you to behave chick."

Beth sighs, realizing she has become too relaxed in her role. She needs to regain her professional, formal attitude; she has grown too emotionally invested in her current assignment. She hopes she hasn't made a huge mistake by allowing herself to become personal friends with her employer. Until now, she hasn't seen this as a conflict.

Four months ago, she packed a suitcase for what she thought would be a week-long vacation in Las Vegas. Thankfully, Marcus had clothing shipped in for her, but now, being home, she packs her own clothing in several suitcases. She also takes time to shop for appropriate beach attire for her return to the island.

Beth has been happy and content in her current position, but her time away helps her recognize she must reel back on interacting as much on the personal side. She plans to do her best work and enjoy it while it lasts. This secluded journey all began when Mancuso asked her to take a chance on a once-in-a-lifetime adventure. One that, on most days, feels less like work and more like a vacation. Beth never imagined the events that followed, but she knows she must remain focused. She can't let Mancuso down.

***

Relaxing in her new townhome, Beth processes a range of emotions. Her thoughts race in multiple directions, but the most vivid is the image of watching a beautiful sunset every night.

Her reflections are interrupted by the sound of her ringing cell phone. Momentarily confused as to who could be calling, she answers mindlessly.

"Hello?"

"Beth, thank goodness you answered! I've been trying to reach you for weeks. Where in the world have you been? I was worried sick."

"Umm, Sammie—hi. I should have called you. Sorry, I took another assignment at a location with no signal."

"Well good for you. I'm just glad you're okay. I had no idea you had taken another assignment."

"Yeah, it was unexpected and in no way planned on my part; it just kinda fell into my path. I only came home to attend to some personal matters, and then I'll be heading back. I apologize. I hope this doesn't put you in a bind."

"No. Honestly Beth, no worries at all. I recently hired a new guy when I couldn't get in touch with you. The reason for my call, isn't about the job, it's because I was concerned for your safety. I was worried about you.

"You're so sweet to be concerned about me, but I'm doing great. So, I take it your writing and recording session was a success? It's only been four months."

"Yes! It was amazing how quickly it all came together. I'm sure you can't share who you're working for now, can you?"

"No, sorry. I can tell you though, that my new assignment is different from any other, but I'm enjoying the change."

"I'm truly happy for you Beth. It sounds like you found something amazing. I wish you only the best. I realize I can be a handful at times, and you always handled me with kindness and grace. I will miss you."

"Good luck Sammie. Thanks again for being concerned about me. If our paths cross in the future, give me a small finger wave, and I'll give you a brief wink."

"You got it Beth. Good luck. I hope to see you around sometime. Toodles."

"Goodbye Sammie."

As she hangs up, she smiles, recognizing that someone out there truly cares about her well-being. It is a good feeling; one she hasn't experienced in years.

As she sits, warmed inside by the knowledge that she has a friend who cares, her thoughts return to the island, especially her nightly walks to watch the sunset. She is surprised by how much she misses the island and her walks to *Sunset Beach*. She misses the warm sand beneath her feet, the sound of Marcus singing and playing his instruments as he composes new material, and the simple companionship of having dinner together every night.

Her life on the island is good, with Marcus and the unlikely duo of men who were a part of the package deal.

Realization hits her hard as she concludes: she misses Marcus.

CHAPTER SEVENTEEN

Three weeks after leaving the island, Beth returns, knowing she must regain her professional footing, though unsure how to do so. She contemplates whether she and Marcus need to have a discussion or if it might cause too much tension. After all, they are isolated, secluded together on the island. She knows she should not have become personally involved. Truthfully, she has grown fond of the relationship they developed, which is unlike her, as she typically avoids crossing professional boundaries.

Her confusion deepens when Marcus meets her at the dock. His words express gladness at her return, but his demeanor screams distance and withdrawal. She immediately notices his indifference, which concerns her, especially since they got along so well before her departure. Is he upset because she stayed away longer than the two weeks she originally requested? During her absence, has he also recognized the need to resume their professional relationship? Has their closeness made them too familiar? Does he realize she was the one who crossed the professional boundary in their employer-employee relationship?

Her mind races with questions as she struggles to understand his new behavior. When she left the island, she thought they had become not just friendly, but friends. They both enjoyed each other's company, but the reality is she is his employee. Perhaps friendship is off the table for them. With his behavior so withdrawn, she feels as though she doesn't know him after all, and maybe she never did. The thought of their newfound distance saddens her.

During her trip, she contemplated what to do; now she decides to focus on discussing professional topics in the future. She tries to engage Marcus in conversation a few times, but his responses are short and flat.

"Yes I'm fine," he says, never expanding or elaborating on his thoughts or continuing the conversation.

She now has genuine concern for him, wondering if his behavior results from her actions or the island's isolation. It has been almost four months since he removed himself from the outside world. Could this have caused depression? Is this why he's withdrawn?

She has many questions but no answers. She plans to continue doing the job she was hired for, giving Marcus his space until he chooses to confide in her again.

After three days of tense interactions, Beth is surprised when Marcus asks if he can accompany her on her nightly walk to *Sunset Beach*.

"Of course, you're always welcome. Nothing would make me happier than for you to join me tonight."

She is elated but confused, as she thought it had become "their" walk before she left for the mainland. She decides not to dwell on the reason, thinking, thank goodness, hopefully this means we're getting back to being relaxed, more ourselves around each other.

The tension has been thick since her return, and she hopes Marcus will open up about what's been on his mind. All Beth wants is to regain the ease of the relationship they had before her visit to the mainland. Perhaps their nightly walk will relax Marcus enough for him to share the reasons for his noticeable indifference towards her.

After dinner, Beth excuses herself; she wants to change into something cooler for the walk. She quickly plans to go for a swim tonight, as she has missed her nightly swims and hasn't enjoyed the ocean since her return from NC. Since Marcus had a storage unit constructed to house towels and other essentials, they sometimes take a relaxing dip before heading back for the night. Tonight, it will be no different.

As they walk to *Sunset Beach*, they engage in light conversation. It isn't their usual casual banter; it's strained but not forced. Beth brings up familiar topics, hoping to make Marcus comfortable.

Focused more on him than the path, she trips over a twig and stumbles. Instinctively, Marcus catches her before she hits the ground, his hands grabbing her waist to break her fall. His touch sends jolts of electricity through her.

Shocked by the sensation, Beth mumbles her gratitude.

"Oh my! Thanks."

Marcus, who also looks shaken, nods with a quiet, "You're welcome."

They continue the walk in silence. Beth can still feel the energy of Marcus's touch on her waist, and Marcus is aware of the sensation lingering in his hands from holding her. Neither is aware of how this interaction has affected the other.

They sit on the sand in silence, watching the sunset as they have many times before. Beth feels Marcus relax as the ocean seems to consume the sun. She knows tonight's sunset is the most beautiful she has ever seen, but then again, she has this same thought every time. Watching the magnificent wonder as the beautiful ball of orange sets over the ocean. Each night is a different vision, one more stunning than the previous experience. Tonight, though, it feels different; her heart skips briefly.

Normally, after the sunsets, they talk for a while before enjoying a magical dip in an ocean glazed with a silver shadow from the moon. They then return to the house feeling refreshed.

When the sun disappears, Beth announces she is skipping their usual routine of chatting in the chaises. Tonight, all she wants is to go directly into the ocean. If she's honest, it's not just the heat; her reaction to Marcus's touch still shakes her. She makes her half-truthful declaration out loud.

"I've missed this nightly routine while I was away and today has been unusually hot."

"That sounds like a great idea. I think I'll join you."

Both strip to their bathing suits and plunge into the refreshing water as the moon continues taking over from the sun. Still feeling an unusual tension between them, Beth decides to swim separately from Marcus. Normally, they stay closer, occasionally splashing each other. Tonight, the thought of doing this feels awkward.

Once refreshed by the cool water, Beth searches for Marcus and motions to him that she's heading back to the beach. As they begin their retreat from the normally calm water; an unnoticed wave crashes behind Beth, knocking her feet out from under her. The powerful force of the wall of water sent her tumbling like a ragdoll to the depth of the shallow beach.

Marcus rushes to help her up, but another wave of water crashes, taking them both down. Marcus is the first to regain his balance and makes his way to help Beth effortlessly to the beach.

Standing in the sand, Beth is mortified at how she must look, feeling like a drowned rat. She's also embarrassed that this is the second time Marcus has rescued her tonight.

Looking up to thank him, she meets his hazel eyes and their concerned gaze. When their eyes lock, neither is able to look away. She feels her breath catch as she tries to speak, but no words come out. Their eyes, however, continue a conversation of their own, one neither of them can prevent. Lost in wordless emotions, with their hearts beating like a drum, they lean in as they find each other's lips.

They are both disoriented, amazed by the hunger and rising heat of the unplanned kiss. Beth feels her knees weaken as the passion sparking between them takes control. With a shiver that is most definitely pleasure , she manages to pull away first and immediately apologizes.

"Wow. Marcus, I don't know what came over me."

"Please don't apologize. I've wanted to know what it felt like to kiss you for a while now. I only realized it after you left the island—and me—for three weeks."

She is mesmerized by his declaration, understanding now why he's been aloof since her return. She listens carefully, absorbing his every word while maintaining eye contact.

"Only then did I realize how much I missed seeing you every day. You've become very important in my life, and I realized how special you are to me. I told myself when you returned, I'd remain distant and not force my feelings on you."

Her mind is overwhelmed, still processing the kiss and the tightness in her chest. She hasn't kissed anyone since Mark, but kissing Marcus feels natural and right. No words are exchanged. She raises her lips to him, intending on a simple kiss in response to his honesty. However, what starts innocently quickly turns passionate, and her calm was shattered with the hunger of his lips. As his tongue traced the soft fullness of her lips, the desire was felt fully by them both.

A delicious shutter heated her body, as they both recognize their emotional bond. Reluctantly, they break apart, ending the breathtaking kiss. After a lingering hug, both feeling centered in the moment, they simultaneously stepped apart.

Marcus was the first to break the silence as they gathered their belongings.

"Welcome home Beth. I missed you."

"I missed you too."

No other words were needed as they returned to the path leading them back to the Triple M. As they walked in silence, each was processing how this unexpected kiss will affect their professional and personal relationship.

In her room, Beth is confused by the new emotions she feels for Marcus. She's his employee, and this wasn't supposed to happen, yet it did, making her want more.

She speaks aloud to herself, "Why do I do these things with Marcus? Things I've never done in my life? And why does it always feel normal when I do them?"

For the next week, Marcus and Beth take their nightly walk to *Sunset Beach*, swim to cool off, and end with a passionate kiss. The heat and intensity grow each time, but it remains only a kiss.

Every night, Beth tries to convince herself their kissing is harmless, just two people seeking a connection, yet she feels she's developing feelings for her boss. She rationalizes their connection, telling herself he's just a nice guy seeking human connection after four months on the island with no outside interaction. She's convenient.

The thought saddens her, but she realizes she too, is seeking a connection. Every night, returning from *Sunset Beach*, she vows it will never go further than a kiss. Her heart twinges as she shakes her head and says aloud,

"Girl, get your head in the game. He is Marcus Donovan, and you're his employee. It's just a kiss or two between consenting adults. Nothing else will come of it."

Yes, he's fighting for his life in the celebrity world, but here on the island, life is different and beautiful. In the real world, she'd be "the help."

Beth reminds herself every morning not to take this further, but as each day progresses, she counts down the minutes until they watch the sunset, swim, and share a kiss before retiring for the night.

CHAPTER EIGHTEEN

Marcus knows he must maintain a professional relationship with Beth, but if he's honest, he's completely smitten. He has been since he first saw her at the interview, when she fell asleep on his shoulder and he carried her to her room.

She intrigued him instantly, and he's been intrigued every day since. He wants to learn more about her and be part of her world. He knows he handled her return poorly, but in fairness, he was unsure of his feelings and needed to work through them.

First, this is a first for him, he has never pursued someone; they always pursued him, making him wary of their intentions. Second, he doesn't want a fling. He doesn't want Beth to think his feelings are because she agreed to be stranded with him on this remote island. She deserves better. She's not a fling to him, and he never wants her to feel convenient.

Lastly, Beth still mourns her husband. Her recent trip home refreshed her grief. It's only been a couple of years, and Marcus doesn't know how much time is enough. He's decided to let Beth choose when, if ever, the time is right to pursue a relationship. The word "relationship" shocks him. Is that what he's seeking?

He knows he must be cautious with both their hearts. He never wants to lose Beth from his life. If she chooses to remain only his employee and friend, he'll respect her decision. The thought of losing her entirely jabs his chest. He must prevent that at all costs.

Their first kiss was spontaneous and unexpected. Marcus was concerned when the waves crashed over her petite form. Scared for her, he reacted. He didn't anticipate the electricity he felt when he carried her to the beach. Initially, he thought it was adrenaline, but when he saw her eyes in the moonlight, his only thought was relief that she was okay. Lost in emotion, his instinct was to kiss her lightly. The purity of the moment was gentle and heartwarming, leading him to ramble about everything he'd tried to avoid since her return.

He never intended to pressure her with his confessions. Her response surprised them both, the passion erupting from a single kiss speaking volumes about what they were afraid to say aloud. His head reminds his heart to give this new dynamic time. He's ecstatic to share nightly kisses, for now. Every day, he counts the hours until their walk, feeling a tightness at the thought of holding and kissing her. He knows he's getting too close and should step back—she's his assistant—but he's drawn to her like a moth to a flame.

CHAPTER NINETEEN

Tonight, as they walk to Sunset Beach, Marcus takes a chance and lightly takes Beth's hand. She doesn't resist. The feel of his hand makes them both gasp; the energy between them is unmistakable. They anticipate how the evening will end, surprised that each night's kisses are more passionate than the last.

Tonight, they decide to swim while the sun sets, a new experience that sounds amazing. Arriving at the beach, they strip to their swimsuits and rush into the water. Beth's mind is a whirlwind of emotion; she needs the cool water to dampen the internal heat growing inside her. She's embarrassed that a simple gesture like holding his hand ignites such passion and desire.

Marcus is first into the ocean. The calm sea should have cooled his desire but seeing Beth's petite form in her bathing suit fans the flames within him. He tries to clear his head; they've swum together before, yet his heart melts, finding her breathtaking. He watches her run gracefully into the water to join him.

They swim and splash each other playfully as the sun sets, feeling free in their private company. Marcus can be himself, without the demands of his career. He enjoys being Marcus, a young man who sings and plays guitar without an audience, with a crush on a girl and acts playful while discerning if she feels the same.

As the waves crash around them, their playfulness leads to kissing. This kiss starts more intensely than the others, their desire instantly evident.

They stumble toward the beach, neither wanting to break the spell, afraid that if they pull away, the magic will be lost for another day. As they fall toward the sand, Marcus breaks away long enough to instruct his watch to turn off all security coverage at *Sunset Beach*. He searches Beth's face for agreement. She nods, kisses his neck lightly, and pulls his mouth back to hers. They both need more than a kiss tonight, recognizing the undeniable passion growing between them.

As Marcus caresses her back and pulls her closer, Beth's mind whirls with the reality of what's about to happen.

"Do you want me to stop?" he asks.

"No, just the opposite."

Marcus's desire skyrockets to heights he never knew existed, and his mind races. He's surprised to feel nervous, an unexpected feeling for him with women. Beth is different; she's important, and he doesn't want to ruin their relationship.

Not that his previous lovers were unimportant, but he feels differently with Beth, unable to explain why. Perhaps he fears examining their situation too closely, worried it might not be real.

Sinking deeper into his passion, he reaches behind her and unties her bathing suit. Overwhelmed by his desire to touch all of her, her breasts are now free, and instinct makes her arch her back for Marcus to hold and kiss them.

He stares into her eyes, seeking permission to continue. Beth places her hands on his face, running her fingers through his hair, gently pulling him toward her breasts. His mouth is like fire, knowing exactly what she wants.

Beth experiences a once-familiar shiver, now unfamiliar until this moment. Her body hasn't forgotten how to respond to desire and knows what she wants. Her mind is in a frenzy as she boldly gestures for Marcus to remove his trunks. She hears him inhale deeply, seeming to share her mindset.

"Hang on there, my little wildcat."

She's losing control, feeling she'll perish if she waits another moment.

"I can't wait; please, Marcus take all of me now."

"Your wish is my command beautiful."

In one rapid motion, he slides her bikini bottom off and caresses her. Beth fumbles to get Marcus naked, shamelessly begging, mumbling, "Please."

Their eyes, glazed with desire, lock as their passion takes over. They make love in the sand on an isolated island under the rising moon, a perfect experience for them both.

Afterward, they lie on their backs, catching their breath. A tear escapes Beth's eye as she whispers, "This was perfect."

Marcus is reeling, his heart full, his eyes fixated on the beautiful woman beside him. He's had lovers, but this feels different. She is different. His heart is now sure that Beth is his soulmate, the one he's been waiting for his entire life. Brushing the tear from her face, the jolt of energy makes him want to make love again.

"Yes, it was perfect."

She snuggles into his arms, resting her head on his shoulder. Marcus feels a familiar relaxation, like the night five months ago, when Beth slept on his shoulder, in his limo, after a long day.

As they bask in the moonlight, he kisses her forehead lightly. She lifts her head to meet his eyes, her mouth quivering. Instinct takes over, and what he intended as a tender act ignites a deep, intense kiss.

Beth runs her hands across his abdomen, daring to explore lower, feeling his sharp breath intake.

"Woman, what are you trying to do to me?"

"I need to know if you're the perfect lover for me or if I've mistakenly got lost in the moment."

"Oh my lady, we are perfect, and I shall enjoy proving it anytime you wish to be reassured."

Without hesitation, he pulls her on top of him, and they become one again. This time, he focuses on pleasing her, mustering all his self-control to take her slowly, wanting tonight to stay imprinted in their minds forever. Here and now, he has no doubt she's his forever. He's been dreaming of exploring her, and now it's happening. He doesn't want to scare her off after one night of lovemaking. This is new territory, so he vows to move slowly and make no demands.

Beth's mind races. She never imagined herself in this situation. A modest, normal girl working security for important people, she's now with the world's most famous man, and he wants her. She tries not to think about a future with him, but every fiber of her being insists he's her missing piece. How did this happen so suddenly? All she can think about is how he makes her feel when he's inside her, and how she wants more. She can't get closer, yet her body craves to be consumed by him.

Marcus notices the confusion on her face, mirrored on his own. He gently rolls her over, needing to have all of her. Using all his energy to remain steady, he begins to shake. Her low, husky command to let ecstasy take over is all he needs as they release together. The aftermath of their second lovemaking is sweeter than the first.

So many emotions consume Beth's mind. Smiling, she thinks she'll sort them out tomorrow; tonight, she's enjoying Marcus's lovemaking. As they lie naked in the sand, she breaks the silence. "Wow."

A few minutes of cuddling and quiet is interrupted by a low ping sound from Marcus's watch. Beth briefly panics, recalling that the entire island is under 24-hour video surveillance, mortified at the thought of someone watching their lovemaking. Marcus recognizes her panic.

"Don't worry; remember, I gave orders to turn off all the cameras before…"

His voice trails off as he glances at his watch; it's a message from the security house asking if they need to reactivate the cameras.

"No," he responds quickly, and her relief is visible. They lie in silence. Beth speaks first, trying to sound casual.

"I guess we'd better get back; I have sand in places I didn't know you could."

She stands, sliding on her sundress cover-up. Marcus puts on his wet, sandy swim trunks. Beth reminds him of the small shower near the entrance.

"I'll be fine to shower back at the Triple M; the walk isn't far."

Holding hands, they walk back in silence. As the house comes into view, Marcus says simply, "On."

Pausing at Beth's room, they share one last kiss for the evening. Both are surprised at how quickly their bodies betray them, wanting more. Marcus mumbles through the intensity, "Join me in my shower."

Beth's sultry eyes and quick nod tell him all he needs to know. They break the kiss only to race to Marcus's room. Inside, he scoops her up and heads to the massive bathroom. Beth giggles, struck by how they're acting like teenagers sneaking somewhere to do grown-up things.

Marcus smiles, his voice raw with emotion as he helps her remove her sundress.

"Let's start by washing the sand off this beautiful body of yours."

He never imagined anything else could take his breath away tonight, but seeing her toned, petite body in the bathroom light, he feels he could explode just looking at her.

"Oh my Beth, you're the most beautiful woman I've ever seen."

Beth blushes, rushing into his arms. How they enter the shower remains a mystery. Marcus, still in his trunks, removes them with her in one quick motion. Soon, they're unable to get close enough. Marcus pulls away; Beth looks confused. He holds a washcloth and soap.

"We have to get this sand off; I can't have your beautiful body all raw and rashy."

As he washes her intimate parts, their eyes lock. Beth follows suit, cleaning sand from him. With the sand gone, she reaches to kiss him, but he touches her lips.

"Wait, hold that thought."

He grabs towels, dries her off, and lifts her into his arms, carrying her to his bed.

"I want this to be a night to remember."

"It already has been for me."

They fall onto the bed, and nothing can stop the tidal wave of raw emotions. The hunger is insatiable; they cling to each other, melting together once again. Beth is sure she has never experienced feelings this profound. The more Marcus gives, the more she wants and needs.

He holds out until he's sure they're both satisfied, and the explosion leaves them dazed and exhausted. Shocked by emotions neither has felt before, Marcus pulls Beth closer. As she lays her head on his chest, he whispers, "Stay with me tonight, in my bed."

They drift into the sweetest, most comfortable slumber.

CHAPTER TWENTY

Marcus awakes, wondering if the night was a dream. Opening his eyes, he sees Beth on the pillow beside him, her arm across his stomach. His desire rises again. It wasn't a dream. He beams, recalling the night in its entirety. Studying her beautiful face, he vows never to pressure her into a relationship but prays she feels as connected to him as he does to her.

Beth, sleeping soundly, senses she's being watched. Slowly opening her eyes, she meets Marcus's gaze. Reading his desire, her own begins to build.

"Good morning."

"Good morning to you too, beautiful," Marcus replies, trying to disguise his husky desire.

Beth leans over, giving him a gentle good morning kiss, already feeling her internal temperature rise. Furrowing her brows, she tries to sound serious.

"Marcus, how will we ever make it through the day when all I have to do is look at you, and I want to make mad, crazy love to you?"

He notices the mix of confusion and desire in her eyes, listening closely as she processes their situation. Her voice trembles as she confesses, "I'm not some sex-deprived teenager, yet making love to you has been the only thing on my mind for the past twelve hours. Please don't think poorly of me, but my body betrays me at the thought of your touch."

Grinning, he feels the same.

"You perfectly said what I couldn't put into words about myself."

The kiss following their confession stirs their internal fires, taking them higher in ecstasy than before. In the aftermath, Beth breaks the silence.

"As much as I hate to say it, it's time to return to my quarters for a shower. Otherwise, we'll never leave this room."

Placing a light kiss on his forehead, she jumps from the bed before he can protest, slips her sundress over her head, and is out the door before he can respond.

Marcus props up in bed, reveling in the feeling of completion from the last twelve hours. He promises himself he'll never hurt Beth or force her into something she's not ready for. She's his soulmate and future, but she must realize this on her own. It's a lot to ask someone to join his chaotic life. He concludes they should continue their daily routine, hoping every night ends at *Sunset Beach*, with her waking up in his bed.

The thought of tonight repeating last night sends a jolt to his loins. He heads for a much-needed, freezing, cold shower.

In her room, Beth hurries to the shower, letting the hot water wash over her as she recalls her body's reaction to Marcus's touch. She's sure she's never felt such overwhelming desire. With just a look from him, she's ready to fall into bed.

It was never this way with Mark; suddenly, she feels she's betraying his memory. She pushes thoughts of Mark away, refusing to compare the relationships. The word "relationship" shocks her. Is that what this is?

Shaking her head, she tries to think clearly, reminding herself it was one night, no matter how amazing. She rationalizes their passion: were they both seeking a human connection? Was the recent tension a factor in the events of last night? Unable to find answers, her confusion builds as she tries to label their relationship. There's that word again.

Beth admits Marcus completes her. He's her missing piece, her soulmate. It's the only explanation for her overwhelming desire. They're an unlikely pairing—he's her boss, an international superstar; she's his assistant. Their worlds are different. No matter how she emphasizes their differences, she wants to be with Marcus. She needs him in her life, always, forever.

She decides to conduct her day as usual. They will work together as they do every day; he hired her to do a job, not sleep with the boss. Unable to control her thoughts, Beth's mind flashes to their nightly walk. Will tonight be a repeat of last night? Her breath catches, anticipating how it will end and whether she'll wake up in his bed.

The hot water hitting her breasts recalls Marcus's tender kisses, making her body moisten.

"Clear your head of last night, Beth. You must work closely with this man today."

She knows what she needs to do, but her body betrays her. Clearing her desire for Marcus is impossible, not today, possibly not ever.

CHAPTER TWENTY ONE

When Marcus arrives in the kitchen for his coffee, right on schedule, Beth has prepared it along with his usual breakfast fruit. She's eaten and is on her second cup. A slight tension lingers as they try to maintain their routine and conversation.

Marcus knows they must keep their distance and proceed as usual. It's difficult not to hold and kiss Beth as he did last night and this morning. Tonight, at *Sunset Beach*, all bets will be off as they explore their intimacy. For now, they must maintain professionalism.

It's Wednesday, and the chef and Rosie, the housekeeper, are arriving soon, so others will be in the house. They must be conscious of avoiding gossip. Also scheduled to join them for a month is Bobby. Marcus expresses concern about Bobby's arrival. Bobby knows him better than anyone and is sharp. They agree to remain friendly, hoping he doesn't notice their newfound desire.

They adjourn to Marcus's office for their daily discussion. Beth takes her usual seat, waiting to discuss their agenda regarding Bobby's awareness of them.

Today, work or planning anything, feels trivial and unimportant. Neither can focus, each knowing the other is reliving their lovemaking. The vividness makes Beth blush slightly. Marcus notices the pink tint, and his heart explodes with knowledge of her desire.

The staff's arrival breaks the tense silence. Bobby suddenly appears in the doorway. Marcus and Beth think they're maintaining indifference, but Bobby, who knows Marcus best, flashes an all-knowing smile.

"I had a feeling this would happen."

Marcus responds quickly, "What? What are you talking about?"

He tries to sound sincere, but they both know what Bobby means. Marcus stumbles for words of denial, but none come. He feels like a teenager caught by his dad with condoms. Beth's face reddens, feeling exposed for doing something inappropriate.

Bobby chuckles, surprising them.

"It's about time. I'm happy for both of you. I knew you'd be a perfect match from the moment I met Beth. I've been waiting for you to figure it out. You're both kind, generous souls. The world is better with you in it. Imagine what you can do as the world's strongest power couple." He grins, adding, "I'm surprised it took this long."

Shocked by Bobby's frankness, they search each other's eyes, seeking answers to unspoken questions.

Was Bobby serious? Did he see them as a couple? A power couple? Marcus gives Beth a reassuring smile, turning to his friend.

"I'm glad you approve buddy. You're correct; we make an awesome pair."

Beth didn't realize she was holding her breath until it burned as it escaped. She feels the need to explain.

"Bobby, you must believe me, I never imagined this happening."

"Well then Beth darling, you're the only one. From the first hour with you, I knew you'd be the perfect one to complete Marcus's life. I believe Marcus knew it too, deep down, the moment you walked into that event like a boss."

Marcus crosses the room to his friend, starting with a handshake that ends in a brotherly hug. Beth hears Marcus's chuckle as he embraces Bobby in admiration. She's still uncertain, watching two close friends express gratitude for their honesty.

As Marcus breaks away, he asks Bobby to join them, shutting the office door. He sits beside Beth. For the next hour, they ask Bobby questions about handling their relationship. That word again. Is that what this is?

"So Bobby, do you think this is happening too fast?" Marcus asks.

"Boss, you're the only one who can answer that. In my opinion, no."

Both notice Beth's rising panic. Bobby reassures her.

"Beth, you can take this as fast or slow as you wish. I believe with all my heart, you're perfect for each other."

Overwhelmed, Beth gathers her thoughts.

"I appreciate your support and honesty Bobby. Yes, there's an unexplainable bond between us, one that is natural and organic, and we don't know how to explain it. It's true; I'm drawn to Marcus, and I never imagined the situation we are in. My concern is that I've only known him as Marcus, not Marcus Donovan, the world-renowned megastar. I'm not sure how I fit into his world."

Though not the response Marcus hoped for, he understands her reservations. His life isn't normal; it's overwhelming, hence his isolation on this island to reevaluate his life and career. He believes he's found what's important: a soulmate. This journey led him to Beth. He'll respect her decision.

Choosing his words carefully, he speaks softly, "You take all the time you need to figure this out; I'll be right here for whatever you decide."

Thankful for his understanding, Beth asks both men to excuse her, as she wishes to retire to her room.

"Take as much time as you need to process our situation. I'll always be here. No pressure."

CHAPTER TWENTY TWO

Entering her room, Beth feels caught in a whirlwind of emotions. Everything is happening at once. She and Marcus don't know where this relationship is going, and now Bobby knows.

She's shocked by his acceptance and approval. Can she trust herself to belong to Marcus? Might he change his mind when he returns to his real life? Is this a mutual attraction, a fling, or could it be something much deeper, real? Long-lasting? Could Marcus be her soulmate? Is this love? It feels like love is beginning to grow. The thought of their relationship sends a wave of desire through her. She needs air, so she grabs a towel and her sunglasses, destination *Sunset Beach.*

She tries to focus on the walk, the island's quiet, and her footsteps on the path. The closer she gets to the beach, the more memories of Marcus flood her mind. She can't escape thoughts of him. She feels his breath on her skin, his tongue on her lips, taking her breath away. Maybe this isn't the best place to clear her head, as her body burns with desire at his memory.

She throws her towel and sunglasses on a chaise and runs to the water. As waves crash around her waist, she cries silently—not from sadness, but from the realization she's fallen in love with Marcus Donovan. He's her soulmate. She can't imagine life without him, nor does she want to. She swims briefly, then heads back to the chaise.

Beth always has a plan; she needs one that works for both of them. Lying in the chaise under the sun, she sets her mind to planning how their relationship can work. After what feels like an eternity, defeated, she concludes she hasn't devised a solid plan, though a few ideas have materialized. Before sharing them with Marcus, she needs to return to the house and write down all possibilities and outcomes.

***

Marcus spends a much-needed day with Bobby. They play pool and walk the grounds, talking about life. Bobby offers encouragement as they discuss Beth, but he mostly listens. Marcus is determined not to pressure Beth into his world; it must be her choice. Bobby feels for his friend, imagining Marcus's heartbreak at finding his forever person, only for her to be scared by his celebrity status.

"She'll accept you, and all the crazy baggage you come with, if your love and bond are truly written in the stars by the Big Guy upstairs. Don't lose hope buddy."

"Thanks man. My life isn't normal, and I'm asking a lot for her to join the madness. Hell, I don't even want to be part of it sometimes."

"A true love will endure it all. Don't give up before giving it a chance to begin."

As evening approaches, Marcus and Beth know there can be no nightly walk with Bobby there. They're weak and will succumb to their desire. They see it in each other's eyes. After dinner and a generic conversation, Beth excuses herself, claiming she needs to retire early. Truthfully, she fears staying longer might lead her to invite Marcus to *Sunset Beach*, knowing they shouldn't.

CHAPTER TWENTY THREE

The next morning, Marcus finds Beth and Bobby in the kitchen, enjoying easy conversation. Both are smiling, and he loves seeing her smile. He watches her quietly, his heart leaping.

Without warning, desire consumes him. He took a cold shower last night and again this morning, dreamed of her, and awoke alone. He must not scare her off; he needs her.

Casually, he announces his arrival. "I hope three is not a crowd for coffee."

Beth meets his eyes with a smile, motioning to his seat where his coffee waits. Okay, it's business as usual, he thinks. He takes a seat, asking how everyone's doing, joining the small talk.

Beth's phone rings, and she excuses herself to answer. Returning after a few minutes, she looks pale and sad. Her tone is flat, trying to sound relieved.

"My house sold."

"How do you feel about that, Beth? Are you sure you're ready?" Marcus asks, knowing it was her dream home with Mark. Selling it means losing another piece of him, turning that part of her life into a memory. Even as time passes, the past hits her hard.

"I know it's the right thing to do; Mark is gone, and that part of my life no longer exists. I can't live in the past; I have a different life now." She pauses, as if to say more, but changes her mind.

Marcus nods, understanding, unsure how to respond verbally. He wonders if things had gone differently in his life, would he be happy?

Beth gathers her thoughts, providing details of the pending sale.

"They want a quick closing, and I need to wrap it up soon. If it's okay, I must return to North Carolina for two weeks."

The glistening in her eyes tells Marcus her heart is breaking, but she's trying to be strong. Both know she's processing the closure of her previous life.

Marcus is sad at the thought of her leaving so soon after they expressed their feelings. He wishes he could go with her, but chooses to respond quickly to avoid seeming like an obstacle.

"Of course, take all the time you need. We'll be right here, waiting for your return."

He extends an offer of assistance, knowing his team has resources.

"Beth, if you need anything, I'm here for you; we are here for you. Just ask."

Marcus strides across the room and embraces her. He feels her quiver and wishes he could take her hurt away. As he releases her, Beth glances at her watch. Today, Rosie and the chef return to the mainland; if she hurries, she can catch the boat.

"Marcus, I'd love to catch New Beginnings back to the mainland this morning, if that's okay. If not, I can put them off until next week."

Marcus nods. "I'll radio down to the dock to let them know you'll join them."

"Thank you Marcus."

Beth hurries to her room, grabbing her suitcase and packing necessities, planning to bring clothing from her condo since she'll be on the island longer.

Marcus insists on accompanying her to the dock. She arrives minutes before the boat departs. In whispers only they can hear, Marcus confesses, "I already miss you and am anxious for your return. Safe travels, and please let us know once you've arrived."

Beth kisses his cheek lightly before heading up the dock to the boat. She gives him a thumbs-up and disappears on board. Once there, she utters words she couldn't say to Marcus without trembling. "I already miss you, too."

CHAPTER TWENTY FOUR

Beth's travel went well; the layovers were short, and thankfully, so were both flights. Once on the ground in North Carolina, Beth contacted the realtor, making an appointment for the following day.

She made a brief stop at her townhouse before heading towards her former home. She needs to say goodbye to this chapter of her life. Beth was sad realizing she was no longer part of the husband-and-wife team that had purchased their forever home.

She entered the home in an unhurried walk feeling the tears daring to fall any minute. The house was empty, except for a few staging pieces she had left behind. She made a mental note to have them removed and placed in storage the next day. Emotionally, today had taken its toll on her—now it wasn't the right time for such a task.

During a final walk-through, she remembered to check the attic. She was glad she did, as she found a few forgotten mementos stored there. They brought back memories of her previous life, and once again, Beth was overwhelmed with emotion. It was a bittersweet reminder that this day truly marked the close of a chapter in her life.

Then she smiled, thinking about the possibility of a new life she could begin with Marcus. She shook her head, telling herself not to let her mind wander there—not today.

When she saw her neighbors, Mike and Carol, returning from the grocery store, she went outside to help them carry their purchases into the house. She would miss this sweet couple who had proven that you could find your soulmate and stay together for fifty years. Seeing them and their evident love gave Beth hope that she could find the same—or possibly, that she already had.

They were delighted to see her and asked if she had experienced any new adventures since they last saw her, a little over a month ago.

She told them things were about the same, nothing new to report and that her employer was great. She hoped they didn't notice the slight pink rise on her neck and cheeks as she thought of Marcus. They didn't seem to notice and was satisfied with her response, not pressing for any more information.

She spent some time visiting, keeping the conversation general. When it came time to say goodbye, it broke her heart to see the couple grow emotional, but Beth refused to say "goodbye," so they agreed on "see you later." The hugs lingered, and a few tears fell before Beth left, heading back to her townhouse.

The next few days were hectic as she arranged for her remaining belongings to be removed and stored with her other possessions. She was surprised to finalize all the negotiations through the realtor rather quickly. The lawyer and closing process, however, was another story. Getting everyone aligned to meet at the same time required her to stay an additional week.

She placed a call to inform Marcus of the situation and make him aware she needed an extra week . He agreed that she needed to stay and see the process through to completion. He hoped she didn't hear the disappointment in his voice; he missed her.

Finally, the house sale was finalized, the buyers were happy, her clothes were packed, her flight was scheduled, and Beth was on her way back to the island three weeks later—with a new plan.

She found she had plenty of downtime while waiting for the inspections and closing to be completed. During that time, she devised a plan—if Marcus agreed. One that would allow them to be a couple without her becoming a target of the media whenever Marcus decided to return to the mainland and resume his celebrity life. She was excited to return to the island and be with him again, to be held by him, loved by him.

***

Traveling back to the island was far from ideal. Both flights were rough, and Beth felt queasy most of the time—both in the air and on the ground. She couldn't shake it off before boarding *New Beginnings*, and the boat ride to the island only worsened her already upset stomach.

Captain Frank, ever the gentleman, offered her Coke and crackers. Beth had never experienced motion sickness before and hoped she would never experience it again. She was mentally and physically exhausted when they finally docked on the island. She had never thrown up this much in her life.

When Beth arrived, Marcus was waiting for her at the dock. The moment he saw her, his heart broke—it was clear she wasn't feeling well.

"I've always heard the expression 'someone looked green,' but now I've seen it firsthand—and I understand."

"It's only motion sickness. Hopefully, now that I'm on solid ground, it'll pass soon."

"Do you normally get motion sickness?"

"No, never. I suppose there's a first time for everything. Honestly, I just need to lie down, if that's okay."

"Yes ma'am. I'll get you settled on the couch and bring you some hot tea and crackers. That should do the trick."

Seeing the concern in his eyes, Beth reassured him she would be fine.

"Truthfully, if someone could stop this merry-go-round and the constant spinning, that would be great."

The tea and crackers helped somewhat, but Beth declined dinner, instead excusing herself in the hope that she could sleep off the dizziness. She was sure she wasn't truly sick—all she needed was a good night's rest to shake off this random spell of nausea and lightheadedness.

Marcus remained concerned. He checked on her several times throughout the night. Each time, he found her sleeping peacefully. He stood quietly by her bedside, wishing he could take away whatever discomfort she was feeling. His heart ached seeing her so fragile. *This must be love,* he thought. He had never wished to take on someone else's illness before.

The next morning, Beth woke still nauseous and dizzy, but she refused to let this "bug" keep her down. She showered, dressed, and applied a touch of makeup to her still-pale complexion before setting out to meet Marcus in their usual morning spot.

Marcus and Bobby were already there, drinking coffee when she walked into the room. Marcus immediately met her eyes, searching for signs of how she felt.

"How are you feeling this morning? I hope you got plenty of much needed rest."

"Thank you for asking. Honestly, I'm still a bit disoriented, but the good news is I feel better than yesterday. And thank you again for the tea and crackers—they were invaluable."

Her eyes met his, and she saw the concern still lingering there. She felt an overwhelming need to reassure him that she was fine.

"I've never had motion sickness before—it doesn't go well with my career choice. I'm still not one hundred percent myself, but I'm a hundred percent better than yesterday. That's an improvement I'll take any day."

Marcus met her halfway with a cup of black coffee and winked as he handed it to her. Their fingers brushed, and the spark that ignited between them was visible in both their eyes.

Beth quickly lowered her gaze, blushing as she remembered the feel of his hands on her body.

"So, what's on the agenda for today? I feel like I've been gone forever."

"It feels like you've been gone forever," Marcus replied softly.

Feeling like the third wheel, Bobby joked, "For Pete's sake, guys, get a room!"

He laughed loudly at his own joke, lightening the mood in the room, and was still chuckling as he made his way to the security house, leaving Beth and Marcus alone.

They discussed a few work matters, then retreated to Marcus's office. Beth tried to focus, but Marcus could tell she still wasn't feeling well. He suggested she go lie down. Beth didn't protest—she excused herself and went to her room, where she stayed for the rest of the day and night.

Once again, Marcus checked on her throughout the night. If she didn't answer his knock, he quietly peeked in to make sure she was okay. Each time, he found her asleep.

By the following morning, her symptoms had eased somewhat. Apart from a few dizzy spells, she felt like she was slowly returning to normal. However, as the days passed, her condition remained unchanged. She ate only small portions at mealtime and went to bed early, feeling unusually tired most of the day.

Marcus grew increasingly worried. Though she kept insisting she felt better, they both knew she didn't look it.

Marcus could tell her complexion was still pale—something she tried to hide with makeup she usually didn't wear.

CHAPTER TWENTY FIVE

She's been back on the island for ten days when Marcus insists she go to the mainland to see a doctor. Beth finds the mere thought of getting on a boat unbearable; even thinking about returning to the water makes her want to heave.

Luckily, Marcus's helicopter arrived while she was in North Carolina. He makes the necessary arrangements for her to be picked up and brought back. He also volunteers to go with her, but Beth assures him she will be fine traveling to and from the mainland alone.

She is beginning to think she has truly picked up a bug during her travels, or it could be a severe case of vertigo. Thankfully, the helicopter ride is short and smooth. Although Beth's stomach does a few flips, she manages to maintain her composure and avoid being sick while in the air—not so much after her feet hit the ground. The pilot looks concerned as she reassures him it's just motion sickness and that she's fine.

***

The doctor is smiling as he enters the room. He's a grandfatherly man with white hair, a slight belly, and a warm smile. Dr. Scott immediately puts Beth at ease. They review her symptoms, what she was doing, and where she was when they started.

"I was sure it was motion sickness at first. Now, I think it might be vertigo—unless I contracted something while traveling."

He listens intently, his eyes kind, and Beth immediately thinks Marcus would like him. After she finishes discussing all her symptoms and concerns, he excuses himself from the exam room, stating he needs to check her lab results.

He returns surprisingly quickly, his smile speaking volumes. Beth is hopeful he has discovered the cause of her symptoms and has a quick-fix treatment.

Without waiting for Dr. Scott to speak, Beth jumps right to the point.

"Will vertigo medication alleviate my symptoms quickly? I have to travel to get home, and I'm already dreading the ride."

Dr. Scott hesitates slightly at her inquiry.

"Beth, it's not vertigo."

Beth is confused for a moment as her mind races with thoughts of a serious illness. Cautiously, she finds the courage to ask, "Is it curable?"

The doctor realizes she's assuming the worst. Seeing fear in her features, he quickly reassures her that she's perfectly healthy.

"Yes dear, you'll be fine. Morning sickness is temporary and should dissipate in a couple of months."

Beth looks confused, but only for a second. Her brain must have misunderstood. What did he say? Morning sickness? Then, the reality of his words registers: she's pregnant.

"I'm pregnant... are you sure?" she whispers in disbelief.

"Yes, it's still very early, so I made sure by double-checking the lab results. We always need to take a second look to confirm, if we think it's an early pregnancy. Yes, you are pregnant. We're estimating about four to five weeks."

Beth knows exactly how far along she is; it's just over four weeks. "I hope this is good news for you," Dr. Scott adds.

Her response is honest and straightforward.

"Honestly, I'm not sure. I've always wanted children, but the relationship is new, and I'm unsure how the father will react. Babies are a blessing from heaven; apparently, I have someone up there who has chosen to bless me. So, yes, I feel extremely happy."

Dr. Scott smiles as he nods. "Yes, they are. I was an obstetrician for most of my career."

"So, what made you switch to family medicine?"

"Babies don't keep a nine-to-five schedule, and I got older."

Beth smiles back, realizing his specialty change was a retirement choice.

Dr. Scott gives Beth advice on various types of home remedies and over-the-counter options to alleviate her symptoms. After leaving his office, she finds a drugstore and purchases a few of the doctor-recommended items before heading back to the helicopter. She opens the ginger candy and prays it works like a miracle and just as quickly. She still has a helicopter ride back to the island.

She is surprised that she already feels different, knowing she's carrying a baby. New mothers often experience sickness, and she knows she can endure morning sickness for this baby. She smiles. They made a baby.

She wonders, what will Marcus say? Will he be happy? Will he feel trapped? Will he trust that it wasn't intentional on her part? These questions rush through her head.

She knows Marcus is very guarded around people. He told her from the beginning that others are always trying to interject themselves into his life. She silently prays Marcus knows the feelings they share are real. Still, everything is moving so quickly. They haven't had the opportunity to discuss their feelings or what a future might look like beyond their pillow talk, and even that wasn't a serious conversation.

The helicopter ride back to the island is brief. Beth is still unsure how to tell Marcus about the doctor's diagnosis. She decides to tell him tonight, after dinner, if she can stomach the meal. She crosses her fingers and hopes for the best.

She decides to take the opportunity to discuss needing a plan for their relationship, should he still choose to have one. She came up with a couple of ideas of how this could work while in North Carolina, but this news might change the dynamics of their relationship.

The pilot must have radioed ahead of her arrival. She notices Marcus waiting for her when they land. Even from this distance , she sees the look of concern on his face. This gives her hope that he genuinely cares about her, and fingers crossed, he will be pleased with the news. She also is aware everything is moving extremely fast, but when you find your soulmate, you accept everything as it should be.

Marcus starts approaching the landing pad as she exits the helicopter. Even from a distance, she sees the concern in his eyes. She wants to run to him, hug him, kiss him, and tell him everything is not only going to be alright, but it will be perfect—or at least that's what she's wishing for. However, she cannot do any of that right now, this is not the time or place, here in front of everyone.

As they meet, Marcus embraces her and places a light kiss on her forehead. He immediately asks what the doctor said and if she's going to be okay.

"Yes, I'll be fine, but it might take a little time."

She didn't intend for her response to sound vague or possibly serious.

The tone of her statement concerns Marcus even more. Afraid to ask, he jumps right to the point.

"Is it something bad?"

Beth, realizing her response sounded like something serious was wrong, adds reassuringly, "No, I'm fine, really, honest. I should be feeling better soon."

Marcus is relieved, but her tone says there is more to it, but he will not press her about it right now.

They turn and begin their walk together towards the Triple M, she smiles, being outside in the sunshine with him feels so good. As they walk, Marcus reaches for Beth's hand, and they continue hand in hand.

Beth feels her heart explode at the warmth of Marcus's touch. Marcus feels relieved when Beth takes his hand and doesn't pull away. He has missed her and her touch so much since the incredible night they found each other.

Beth breaks the silence.

"Is Bobby still on the island? I feel so out of touch these days."

"Yes, but I believe he's scheduled to leave tomorrow." Marcus answers, his mind still focused on Beth and her health.

"Good. I'd love to discuss something with you both after dinner tonight, if that's okay with you."

She makes this statement without hinting at the reason for wanting to speak to them both simultaneously.

"OK...I was hoping for some time alone with you, but yeah, I'll let Bobby know. I still haven't figured out how my best friend is your biggest fan."

"It's because he has great taste."

Marcus leans down and whispers in her ear, "I think we both have great taste, personally."

She feels his warm breath on her neck, reminding her of their kisses and sending shivers down her spine. For an instant, she considers throwing caution to the wind and professing her love to him here and now. Thankfully she doesn't and she comes to her senses, knowing this isn't the time or place.

"You better behave yourself Marcus Allen Donovan. You know what happens when you get too close to me."

She laughs at his expression when she uses his full name. He has a look of amusement, and for a brief instant, she thinks she can see love in his eyes—not just desire, but actual love for her.

Could this be? Is she only seeing what she hopes to see?

She quickly changes the subject.

"If it's okay with you, I need to retire to my room before dinner."

As she walked away she heard him say softly,

"Definitely. I'm glad you'll be okay. I care about you Beth, a lot."

CHAPTER TWENTY SIX

Once in the solitude of her room, Beth tries to decide how to tell Marcus and Bobby about her condition: that they created a beautiful baby. She prays all will go as it should, but she must admit she's unsure exactly what to expect. She's certain of one thing: this is unexpected news and they'll both be shocked.

She paces the room, composing and rehearsing a speech on how to break the news. She plans to appear nonchalant and neutral. Her rehearsal is interrupted by a light knock on her door; it's Bobby.

"So, you're back. Marcus said you asked him about me? What predicament have you gotten yourself into young lady?"

"I wasn't 'looking' for you. I only asked him if you were still on the island. The past few weeks have been a blur; I am not sure who is doing what these days. Anyway he said you were. I told him I wanted to talk to you both later, after dinner."

Bobby gives her one of his mischievous smiles as he rubs his chin.

"I think you need to tell Marcus about your pregnancy alone. You don't need me as an audience. Three is a crowd in these conversations."

Startled by his words, Beth is sure her face, already green from nausea, turns ghost white. She tries to form a coherent sentence.

"Wait. What? Wha…How do you know?"

He's unsure exactly what color she turns; at first, she seemed pale, then white, but now her face is turning red as she confronts him with broken words. Bobby just smiles, responding,

"Well, Marcus is naive; I, on the other hand, not so much. You have had motion sickness for weeks; sorry, but it doesn't normally work like that. So, it was a simple deduction on my part. Seeing how you've found comfort in each other's arms—finally, with my approval I might add—pregnancy is my final answer."

He notices when a small tear escapes from Beth's eye and runs down her cheek. For a moment he is sad that his teasing did not seem to ease her tension.

"Do you think he's going to hate me? Will he think I'm trying to force him into a commitment? I can't bear the thought of him being upset or angry with me. I promise none of this was intentional. This is so unexpected. Oh Bobby, what happens now?"

"I doubt he'll be any of the things you mentioned, but we can't guess or presume how he'll react until you tell him."

Bobby is making a valid point; she won't know how Marcus feels until he knows.

"I'm telling him tonight. I was going to tell you both at the same time, but here you are, guessing correctly. I was hoping to have you as a buffer. Marcus may need a friend."

Her mind is reeling; she now needs a new strategy for how to share this shocking but beautiful news.

"Do you think we should walk to *Sunset Beach*? We can talk privately there; after all, it's where it all started."

She tries to smile as she says it, but Bobby can see she's nervous about how Marcus will take the news. He crosses the room and hugs her tightly.

"It'll all work out. Don't worry so much; it's not good for the baby. A walk to the beach sounds like exactly what you both need."

He kisses her lightly on the cheek and turns to exit the room. When he reaches the door, he turns back towards her.

"Congratulations from Chloe and me. She's the one who really figured it out; truthfully, I'm just as clueless as Marcus."

He chuckles at his own ruse as he leaves the room, closing the door behind him.

***

Beth must now regroup her strategy for sharing their new predicament. Now she is experiencing various emotions in anticipation of the nightly walk with Marcus. When she feels unsure, thinking things may not go as she hopes, she remembers Bobby's words of comfort. Then she also has thoughts of it going perfectly and how the night might end.

Bobby said he was excited for them and doesn't seem concerned about Marcus's reaction. She puts her faith in Bobby; he knows Marcus better and longer than anyone. She feels confident he would tell her if he thought Marcus might respond negatively.

Beth stays confined to her room, waiting for dinner. Her emotions are everywhere. Her heart leaps with memories of their one night together. They created this little human growing inside her on one of the best nights of her life. She hopes Marcus feels the same.

She's unsure what the future holds or if there even is a future for them. All she knows is that she has fallen madly and deeply in love with Marcus Donovan and is carrying his child. They'll always be connected, even if he rejects her. She realizes she has no idea how this will work out, but knows she'll accept his reaction, whatever it is.

She continually glances at the clock, mentally counting the minutes until dinner. She's thankful for Dr. Scott's remedies and hopes they limit her morning sickness to mornings. At this moment, her only prayer is to make it through dinner. Getting sick tonight isn't an option.

Beth chooses one of the new outfits she purchased in North Carolina. It's cool and comfortable, perfect for their dinner and beach walk afterward. She places her hand on her flat stomach, still surprised to know a baby is growing inside her.

She thinks about what raising a baby with Marcus might look like. She imagines him as a loving father. He's a kind and gentle man, and she's sure he'll make an excellent dad. No matter what the outcome between them, she knows both parents will love this baby.

Her mind then rushes to negative thoughts and scenarios. How can Marcus be there for her and the baby when he returns to touring the world? He would be gone for extended periods of time, leaving her alone. How does this pregnancy affect her job? How would she and the baby survive if she didn't have a job? What kind of job could she find with a good income? Beth realizes that she now has responsibilities beyond herself. It's all overwhelming.

In her mind, she hears her mother's voice:

"Don't put the cart before the horse Beth."

"I know Mom," she whispers aloud as she runs to the bathroom with a wave of nausea.

As she prepares to join Marcus for dinner, she feels better, and hopes this feeling continues throughout the night. Nothing can interfere or ruin her evening with Marcus. Tonight, her world will change one way or another. She mentally prepares for his reaction. She crosses her fingers, praying for a positive outcome as she exits her room.

Beth enters the dining room to find Marcus staring out the window, deep in thought.

"Hi stranger," she manages to say without her voice cracking.

Marcus turns; he'll never be accustomed to how beautiful she is. He knows she still doesn't feel well, but she's glowing, and she looks perfect to him.

"I trust you got some rest and are feeling better tonight."

Beth, not trusting her voice, only nods and smiles.

Marcus has set the table and warmed the food the chef left for them. Beth feels spoiled and tells him so. He grins and crosses the floor to where she stands. When he reaches for her hand, she automatically gives it to him. He guides her to her chair and adjusts it once she's seated. He then sits beside her, never taking his eyes from hers.

They attempt light conversation about the island's day-to-day events while she was away. Marcus shares that he's struggling with new material but is optimistic it'll come together soon.

He also tells her that Bobby chose to bow out of dinner and hopes they can still have the discussion she requested. Beth nods, explaining that Bobby visited her room earlier and begged off, not wanting to be a third wheel in their conversation.

Neither eats much, each for different reasons, as the anticipation of the night is too great.

Beth suggests they walk to *Sunset Beach* and talk along the way. Marcus smiles, agreeing it's an excellent idea.

CHAPTER TWENTY SEVEN

As they begin their journey down the path to their special beach, Marcus reaches for Beth's hand, and she instinctively and naturally gives it to him. They continue walking in silence to their spot on the sand, ready to watch the sunset, as they've done many times. Marcus places his arm around Beth's waist, and she leans into him. They sit silently as the brilliant orange sun disappears into the ocean, both swearing this one is more beautiful than any they've witnessed before. Still in awe, they remain quiet and still as the moon begins its journey into the night sky.

Now nervous and unsure how to start her much-needed conversation with Marcus, with all her rehearsed words gone, she blurts out her secret.

"Marcus I'm pregnant."

Holding her breath, she waits for his response.

His arm around her waist tightens as he pulls her closer. She turns to search his eyes in the moonlight and notices a faint glistening forming in them. He releases her waist and cups her face with both hands, kissing her gently. Within moments, the simple gesture escalates to one of deep passion. The desire is unmistakable. Breathless, Beth is the first to break away.

"Did you understand what I said?"

"Yes, and it's the best news I've ever heard in my life. Now, can I continue kissing you?"

Once again, they get lost in the taste of longing for each other. This kiss has been long overdue, and they both recognize the growing need to explore their building desire for more.

They pause long enough to agree to return to the Triple M. They reluctantly break free from one another, they hastily return to the mansion, where they intend to continue their lovemaking in Marcus's suite. They are both giddy with anticipation as they enter the massive doors. Upon entering, Marcus turns to Beth, locks eyes with her, and states proudly,

"I love you Beth White. I knew you were special the first time I laid eyes on you. I've been waiting my entire life for you."

Beth melts on the inside as he takes in the sweetness of her lips one more time. He reaches down, lifts her into his arms, and effortlessly carries her up the grand staircase to his bedroom suite.

Once inside, all bets are off as they undress each other in a frenzy. The need for their bodies to touch unobstructed is unstoppable. Once all their clothing is discarded, they fall into bed, and Marcus makes them one again without hesitation.

They kiss each other hungrily as their bodies rock to the sound of the waves they hear in the distance. The only other sounds are deep breathing and an occasional low moan of ecstasy.

When Beth feels she can't wait another second, she commands Marcus to extinguish her fire with his release. Without hesitation, he complies, and they both peak, quivering in complete satisfaction.

In the aftermath, they lie in each other's arms, with Marcus gently caressing her back and her head on his chest.

"I love you too Marcus."

He gently kisses the top of her head and replies,

"It's a good thing, because I surely don't want to survive in this world without you in mine."

Grinning, he reaches his hand out and touches her flat stomach.

"You are my greatest blessing in life Beth; besides your love, you now give me the best gift imaginable."

As they lie tangled together, they decide to discuss plans and options in the morning. Tonight is theirs. Here and now, expressing their love to one another is the most important.

Beth nestles against Marcus's neck, kissing his jawline and ears. Feeling bold, she allows her hand to travel to the lower region of his belly. He lets out a slight growl as he warns her teasingly,

"You'd best be careful young lady; I can't be held responsible."

Her hand continues, and as promised, another round of lovemaking ensues.

When both are satisfied and regaining their senses, Marcus wonders if he'll ever get enough of this little spitfire, this amazing woman he has fallen completely head over heels in love with.

The pair is feeling totally relaxed, Beth is resting in the comfort of his arms, as they drift off into a peaceful night of much-needed slumber.

***

Beth awakes to find Marcus standing across the room, staring out the large window that consumes the entire wall, watching the ocean.

"Good morning Daddy."

He turns and replies in the same playful banter.

"Good morning Mommy."

His long legs cross the room quickly, and he falls back into the bed, kissing Beth intently. As things begin to heat up, both recognize how quickly the kiss is escalating beyond a simple good morning greeting. Marcus breaks free and mumbles against his will.

"Sorry darling, as much as it pains me to say this, not this morning. I must see Bobby off the island in an hour."

At the mention of Bobby's name, Beth's face goes pale in an instant.

"Oh no! You didn't give instructions to turn the cameras off at the beach last night."

Marcus is also shocked at the realization, but his main concern is for Beth. He knows she wants to maintain their privacy, even though it was just a kiss. No, not just kissing. As the memories flood back, Marcus recalls the groping, grinding, and petting that occurred after her pregnancy announcement.

"I'll see Bobby right away. I'll have the footage deleted. We both know we can trust him."

Since he had gotten up early to shower and was already dressed, he darts out the door on a mission to protect his beautiful woman from exploitation.

***

Marcus arrives at the security house and upon entering, calls out loudly to Bobby as he makes his way to his room.

Bobby hears him when he enters the house and notices he sounds frantic as he yells for him. He's on his way out of his bedroom, suitcase in hand, as Marcus enters the doorway with a harried look in his eyes.

"Good morning Boss. What's up?"

Marcus who has no time for pleasantries, begins blurting out, "The *Sunset Beach* footage from last night needs to be erased right now, and please tell me you haven't already seen it."

Bobby smiles as he raises his hand for Marcus to take a breath.

"Breathe man. Don't worry, the cameras were never on— Daddy."

Marcus, realizing what Bobby just said, questions him. "She told you before she told me?"

"Nah, relax brother. Chloe guessed by her symptoms, and Beth confirmed it. That's why I bowed out of the meeting she wanted with us."

Marcus feels a wave of relief, as if a weight has been lifted; he was on a mission to save Beth from embarrassment. His dear friend had the insight to turn the cameras off. For the first time since hearing about Beth's pregnancy, Marcus gets emotional with his beloved friend. His eyes begin to tear up.

"Bobby, she's having our baby— my baby."

"Congratulations boss man. You're perfect for each other, and I wish you and Beth all the happiness in the world. Have you considered what happens next? How will this relationship be handled?"

"Recently, I've been daydreaming about what the future would look like with Beth. I never imagined it would truly happen or fathomed our current situation. I'm overjoyed and excited about this new chapter of our lives. My life has a new beginning with Beth by my side."

Bobby approaches Marcus and hugs him.

"You both will make awesome parents. I'm genuinely happy for you both. I only ask that you ensure you will always take care of her—not because she's the mother of your child, but because she's your world."

"Bobby, you know I've always trusted you to guide me in the right direction. Today, I need your help with a few urgent things. Will I be a terrible friend if I ask you to stay for a couple more days? I can't navigate what I'm planning on my own. I promise I'll make it up to you and Chloe."

Bobby is enjoying this version of Marcus. He's excited about planning his future. He hasn't seen him this excited or show this much interest in his life in a long while. All he knows is that Marcus is happy, which makes him glad, too.

With complete honesty and seriousness, Bobby states,

"It's always my pleasure to assist you whenever and wherever you need me. Of course, I'll stay for as long as you need buddy. Just so you know though, Chloe will be expecting to attend the wedding, just a heads up."

The two old friends laugh as they shake hands, leading to another hearty embrace and exchanging words of true friendship.

Marcus and Bobby know Mancuso should be arriving any minute for the monthly switch. They wait patiently at the security house for his arrival. Mancuso senses something is amiss, as both look anxious when he enters.

"Okay, this looks like trouble brewing. What gives?"

The two embark on the story of Marcus and Beth's involvement, ending with the news of her pregnancy.

"So, Mancuso you know how Beth and Marcus seem to work so well together? Well— apparently they have been doing a little kissy face, among other things and now they have a 'surprise'"

"Bobby stop! You make it sound like a fling, it's not! Tony, Beth and I have realized we are in love, I am so thankful you invited her to the hiring event. Anyway, we had a couple intimate moments and now she is expecting our child."

He prayed Mancuso would approve of them as a couple and as parents. When Marcus finished speaking, he was nervous as he waited patiently for his response.

Marcus is shocked when Tony unexpectantly states he's not surprised to learn that a love connection had developed between them. He repeats, almost word for word, what Bobby said, emphasizing how they're perfect for each other and make an incredible power couple.

His reaction to the pregnancy news, however, isn't as approving as Bobby's. His initial response is concern for Beth. He wants to protect her. With his features stern, he begins in a low and serious tone, as he speaks to Marcus.

"I'm going to be straight with you. Beth is important to me. We have a long history. I consider her my family. You better not ever hurt my girl. I mean it, Marcus, not ever. I know she's tough and trained to protect, but you better always protect her. Promise me."

Marcus understands Tony's words clearly, as well as the underlying threat.

"I promise, you don't have anything to worry about Tony. She will always be safe with me. I love her; she's my entire world. I've waited my whole life for her. My mission in life will always be to protect her and our child."

"Says the man who has not one, not two, but three security detail employees." Bobby interjects playfully.

"Dude stop trying to 'help' me out with Beth's honorary daddy stand-in. You are not helping."

Mancuso shakes his head at their continual jabs towards each other. He knows it is a game Bobby plays to help Marcus through difficult situations.

"OK you two. Contrary to what Bobby thinks, I fully understood the sentiment behind Marcus's words of intent."

"Thanks Tony. Your approval of our situation is important to me. What I said was the truth, I would put my life on the line for her every time."

It was only after hearing Marcus's oath of love and protection, does Mancuso congratulate him.

"Congratulations on finding true love and your forever person. You have chosen a wonderful lady to fall in love with. Welcome to the family, I guess according to Bobby, I am now your fill-in father-in-law. I'm excited to watch your love story bloom and grow as you welcome a new tiny human to our family."

"You are both welcome for my input." Bobby says, laughing at his own joke.

* * *

This small group of three men work together for the next few hours helping Marcus develop and execute a proper proposal and subsequent wedding.

With John's help, they use the security house monitors to view hundreds of rings online until Marcus chooses the perfect one for Beth.

Next, John places multiple phone calls to various jewelers checking who has it in stock. He then arranges for payment and store pickup. Luckily, the jewelry store isn't too far inland, and Mancuso agrees to take the helicopter and retrieve it for Marcus.

They were not surprised when Marcus tells them he wants the proposal to be tonight, with the wedding taking place within two to three days, if Beth agrees. He's anxious to claim her as his, and the sooner, the better.

With the ring secured, next on the list is location. Bobby and Marcus search for the perfect location to perform a private, legal marriage ceremony.

Bobby asks Marcus if he would rather fly an officiant to them, but Marcus declines. This is their spot, their island. The thought of letting an outsider into their world isn't what he wants. Also, he wants this to be a special getaway with a honeymoon suite.

Bobby finds a lovely spot, on a nearby island, and with some negotiating, reserves the entire hotel for the day after tomorrow. Bobby chuckles, knowing the money he offered to the hotel and officiant, didn't hurt in their eager acceptance.

Next on the list, wedding attire for both, to be purchased tomorrow. Bobby confirms all the arrangements for Beth and Marcus. He agrees to accompany Beth to the mainland to shop for the perfect dress. With an extra monetary incentive, he easily manages to get the shop to agree to close and cater to Beth's needs. They're notified there's no budget; he only requires a happy bride. Once again, money makes anything happen.

He then focuses on Marcus. Mancuso will accompany him on his mission to find the perfect outfit for the beach wedding. Marcus knows what he wants; he only hopes he can find it.

All the details and arrangements appear to have fallen in place, seamlessly. Marcus now turns his focus on the most important part, the proposal, the only missing piece to the puzzle. Well, not exactly the only missing piece—Beth still needs to say yes and agree to the quickness of the nuptials.

Once again, as in most instances, those closest to Marcus understand his urgency. The quicker things happen; the less likely word leaks out and exposes the parts of his life he chooses to keep private.

Bobby keeps in constant contact with Chloe all day, concerning the arrangements. She's thrilled when Marcus invites her to join them for the ceremony. She hasn't met Beth face-to-face; they've only spoken several times by telephone.

Since Bobby's initial meeting with Beth in Las Vegas, he's shared so much about her, almost nonstop, that Chloe feels she knows her. From what Bobby has told her about the dynamics between Marcus and Beth, they sound like a perfect match.

"Thanks boss for including Chloe, I didn't want to say it earlier, but I could really use her help in the whole dress shopping ordeal. I know you want your bride to be beautiful, but I can't say with certainty it would have happened with me. Unfortunately, I don't have your fashion sense."

"Of course Chloe is invited! She is family, and since I can't have my parents here, you, Chloe and Tony are all we both have. Besides, remember I am her favorite person."

"Yes you are boss, yes you are. Still not sure how that happened."

"Another thing, I don't think you would hold much clout as my security guard if you dressed like me"

"How right you are buddy! Could you imagine me dressed like you? Sorry, but not in this lifetime, or the next for that matter."

"Whoa…what's wrong with the way I dress?"

Bobby was making a faux face of disapproval.

"One word, FLASHY."

"OK, I have to agree but look at the money it has made me."

"Well, there is that, as well as you have a brilliant talent, and your voice is phenomenal."

"Awe thanks. Here I thought you no longer cared about me."

Bobby was enjoying the playful banter between him and Marcus. Beth brought out a side of Marcus that fame had taken away.

"You are stuck with me forever boss, I am not going anywhere. I am happy for you and this new chapter of your life."

It's mid-afternoon when the helicopter returns with Mancuso and the most beautiful ring Marcus has ever seen. The pictures did not do it justice, it is stunning. He can't wait to see it on Beth's hand. He is counting down the hours until their sunset walk tonight.

Marcus discusses wanting to propose where the cameras can capture the entire event. He knows Beth will want this memory recorded, she is sentimental that way. Without a doubt, he trusts Bobby, Tony, and John to only record the proposal and nothing more.

The three men of the security team are excited when Marcus gives them permission to watch the proposal live. John is in awe when he's also included. Witnessing this huge, worldwide secret is an honor. Marcus and Beth are special to them all, and they wish them both a lifetime of happiness.

CHAPTER TWENTY EIGHT

Dinner is unusually quiet for both, each for different reasons. Beth thinks she's giving Marcus space to process the news about the baby. She knows he spent most of the day with Bobby and Mancuso. She's curious about why Bobby is still on the island but thinks it's best to ask tomorrow when Marcus is ready to share.

After dinner, they embark on their nightly walk. Beth takes Marcus's hand and squeezes it tightly. When their eyes meet, they both feel the undeniable love between them. They continue their walk in silence.

Just before reaching the beach, Marcus drops her hand and stops. When she looks to see the reason, she catches him as he goes down to one knee. At first, Beth is confused, not understanding. Marcus sees the moment of realization on her face as she notices the glisten of the ring he holds out to her. He prepared all day what he would say, but now, in the moment, he forgets it all. He speaks from his heart.

"Beth, I know this is sudden, but when you find your soulmate, your true love, there's no need to wait. I've dreamt about you my entire life. I love your strength and determination. I love how you accept me for who I am. I miss you when you're away. I can see our future. You are perfect for me, and we are perfect for each other. We created a new life from our love. I love you. Will you marry me?"

Beth is so unsuspecting and unprepared. She's spent the last two days hoping and praying Marcus wouldn't feel trapped or upset about their situation. She worried about raising their baby alone if he rejected her. Now, here he is before her, on one knee, proposing.

She is elated. She has no doubts she loves Marcus or that he's her soulmate until the end of their days. Without hesitation, through the happy tears of love forming in her eyes, in a voice full of nothing but true love, she says,

"Yes. Yes, Marcus, I'll marry you."

Marcus, also fighting back emotional tears, rises to his feet and claims her mouth. What starts as a gentle confirmation of their union quickly turns into a passionate kiss of hunger fueled by desire.

Marcus reluctantly pulls away, adding, "Just one more thing. I want to get married as soon as possible. I've already made plans if you said yes. Everything is arranged for the day after tomorrow. Please understand my urgency, and don't be upset."

Beth is giddy; she's marrying this remarkable man, and the sooner, the better.

"Sounds good to me, but what do you want me to wear?"

Marcus laughs as he answers jokingly, "I prefer it when you wear nothing, but I'm not sure how the wedding photos will turn out."

His true statement makes Beth laugh, and she gives him a playful nudge, calling him silly.

She tells him about her shopping trip in North Carolina, saying she can wear one of her new dresses. Truthfully, she couldn't care less about what she wears; she's just happy to be marrying the man she's fallen in love with and carrying his child.

Proudly, he announces that the sky's the limit, only the best for his beautiful bride.

"Bobby has already contacted a boutique on the mainland to assist you in finding the perfect dress. Neither of them liked my vote on less clothing."

"I like your vote. Maybe not for the wedding but now isn't a bad time to get your approval."

They seal their commitment with an enthusiastic kiss. Marcus pauses long enough to tell his watch, "Stop." The recording has gone far enough, and he's sure they're both about to be in a steamy situation—one that will leave them with less clothing.

***

Beth wakes anxious for the day ahead. Today, she'll try on beautiful dresses to find the perfect one for her wedding day. Tomorrow, she'll marry the man of her dreams, Marcus; it's still unbelievable to her.

She reflects on this beautiful life they're about to embark on, taking a moment to smile and think that all this is happening because she took a last-minute red-eye to Las Vegas less than six months ago. She can barely remember her life before Marcus. She shakes her head and, checking the clock, realizes she has no time to reminisce.

She returned to her room last night after another amazing night of lovemaking. Marcus asked her to stay as she had before, but Beth knew they both needed rest, as the next couple of days would be busy. He reluctantly agreed she was right for them to sleep alone; however, the desire in his eyes told her he wasn't thrilled with the idea.

She quickly showers and gets dressed. She's forever thankful for the ginger candy, as it helps alleviate her nausea. She makes a mental note to get more on the mainland. She also says a silent thank you for their existence every time she puts one in her mouth.

She arrives at the heliport and finds Marcus, Mancuso, and Bobby waiting. Afraid she's running late; she glances at her watch. By her calculations, she's ahead of schedule.

"Sorry if you've been waiting a long time. I didn't think I was late."

Bobby, pointing at Marcus, is quick with his usual banter. "We've been waiting, but by no fault of yours. If he'd had his way, we would've left at 4 a.m. when he got up."

Marcus smiles as he approaches Beth.

"Good morning my love. Yeah, I was lonely." He takes her in his arms and kisses her lightly.

"Oh no! Now we'll never leave. Enough with the mushy stuff you two," Bobby says from behind them, making them all laugh. Marcus and Beth love to hear Bobby's teasing, and they know he not only approves of but was apparently hoping for their current relationship—well, minus the added bonus of a baby.

Marcus helps Beth into the helicopter before taking his seat beside her. They put on their headphones and prepare for the short ride. Marcus reaches for her hand, which she accepts with a smile. As they begin the flight, he squeezes her hand and silently mouths, "I love you Beth."

She smiles in return and repeats his silent mouthing back to him. "Ditto I love you, but even more."

He raises her hand to his lips as he says, "Never."

***

The plan is for them to go their separate ways once they arrive on the mainland. Marcus will fly somewhere on the jet with Mancuso, to an undisclosed location, to retrieve his wedding attire. Meanwhile, Bobby will transport Beth to the boutique he arranged for the day.

After landing, they embrace and share a simple kiss before proceeding to their designated SUVs.

"See you later. I hope you find the perfect outfit; we both know you have excellent taste in clothing."

"I already have everything a man could ever want, but I wish for you to find your dream dress. Remember, the sky's the limit. Love you and enjoy your day."

Bobby walks ahead of Beth toward the SUV and opens the back passenger door for her to get in. She's about to protest, reminding him she likes to ride shotgun, when he stops her.

"Sorry Beth, but someone has already claimed your shotgun position today."

Only then does Beth notice the brunette sitting in the front passenger seat. She quickly decides to engage in friendly banter with Bobby.

"Yep, I see her. I hope you don't think she's also a perfect match for Marcus."

They both explode into laughter at her quick jab about their first encounter.

"Touché. Nope Beth, this one's all mine."

She hears the pride in his voice; then the realization hits her: this is Chloe.

"Oh my! Well hello! Nobody told me you were coming today. I'm thrilled to finally meet you. I'm so happy to have you here and part of my special day."

Chloe can't take her eyes off the beautiful blonde in the backseat. She's barely able to contain her excitement.

"There was no way I'd have missed Marcus getting married. I'm thankful he invited me. Well, I may have demanded it. Seriously Beth, I'm happy to finally meet you face-to-face. Congratulations. I'm here to help you in any way possible."

Bobby interrupts briefly, feeling the need to explain.

"I hope this is okay with you Beth. Marcus and I figured you could use some female companionship in dress shopping. Chloe's the better choice with all the girlie stuff than me."

The comment makes both ladies laugh as Chloe confirms his statement with a nod.

"True story, he has no fashion sense."

"Besides, it's time you both get to know each other. What better time than now? After all, one day you'll be neighbors in Oklahoma." He disregards Chloe's comment about his fashion sense.

Chloe's expression suddenly changes as she realizes Beth was unaware of her arrival.

"Bobby, why didn't you tell her I was going to be here today?"

She turns to Beth and asks with genuine sincerity, "I hope you don't mind my unexpected visit or think of me as an intrusion on your special day of finding your dream dress."

"Oh my gosh sweetie, not at all!. I'm happy y'all thought to be here for me. I'm grateful to have someone else's opinion. You know, I normally wear a lot of black and grey. Hon, I also consider it an advantage since you know Marcus well and can give me insight into what he might like."

Bobby and Chloe exchange glances when they hear Beth slip back into her Southern accent along with the slang.

"Well I'll be! Has Marcus heard that accent?" Bobby asks.

Chloe jumps in to defend Beth.

"Bobby Simmons, you stop teasing her right now. I find it adorable."

Beth can't help but laugh at both of them as well as herself. Over the years, she's been away from home so much that her accent has mostly faded. However, every now and then, it sneaks out. She decides to have a little fun and be full-blown Southern when she responds.

"Darlin's, don't y'all know it ain't nice to make fun of a li'l ole Southern gal?"

All three occupants of the SUV burst out laughing.

"Well sir! You really are a true Carolina girl," Bobby says.

"Yes sirree bob, every now and then ya gotta get back to yer roots."

Chloe is laughing so hard she's begging Beth to stop.

"Girl, I see why everyone loves you. You're a remarkably interesting young lady. I think we'll become best friends; you are my people."

When they park in front of the boutique, Bobby states matter-of-factly that he'll return later.

"We've arrived ladies. Go have fun and call me when you've found your perfect dresses." He appears relieved to have dodged the dress-shopping bullet.

"I'm going to see if I can find a hole-in-the-wall with a pool table and a cold beer."

They know Bobby is an unsuspecting pool shark and briefly feel sorry for his would-be opponents. Chloe shoots him a warning look.

"Robert, please don't take all their money today; play nice."

"Don't worry darling, I'll leave them with enough change for cab fare, but I plan to have a little 'ching-ching' when I return, so you can also have a pretty new dress today."

"Sweetheart, I was planning on a new dress today, whether you play pool or not."

She leans across to kiss him on the cheek and shifts her gaze to the backseat.

"Come on Beth, we have some money to spend." She opens her door and gets out of the SUV.

Beth hears Bobby mumble and knows by his tone, that he's teasing.

"Guess I need to find an extra target or two so I can win a few more games."

Beth smiles. She's in awe of their easy and loving relationship and hopes she and Marcus can have the same.

***

Beth is sure she's never seen so many beautiful dresses in one place. All the dresses in the small boutique are designer status. The sales ladies are extremely nice as they engage with Beth and Chloe, inquiring about their styles. Marie is the clerk assigned to be Beth's assistant for the day.

Beth is unsure of the style but states she doesn't want to wear white. Everyone is surprised by this revelation and convinces her to try on a few white dresses anyway. She hates to admit it, but they all look great on her, and she begins to rethink her objection to white.

Then she sees it. A gorgeous pink dress catches her attention from across the room. She's unable to see all the details, but what she sees intrigues her. It's as if it's calling out to her.

It's simple yet elegant, light and airy, perfect for a beach wedding. The high empire neckline is modest, with just enough sparkles and shirring to make it magical. Yet, it has a sheer bodice, giving it the slight touch of the sexy vibe she wants. Beth has always enjoyed a hi-lo hem, and this dress doesn't disappoint. The hem has wisps of feather-like tulle. Overall, it's gorgeous.

She's anxious to try it on immediately. Marie, the salesclerk, is shocked when Beth asks for the dress to be retrieved and brought to the fitting room. As Beth steps into the pink dress, she knows instantly it's the perfect dress—her wedding dress.

Marie is speechless; the dress is beautiful on Beth. To her surprise, it fits perfectly, as if it was designed especially for her and was waiting for her to choose it. Marie has been assisting with wedding dresses for years and has never had a bride take her breath away—until today. She's speechless when she looks at this beautiful pink vision standing in front of her. As she searches Beth's face, they both know this is the dress. Beth is glowing. She twirls, asking Marie to confirm what they both already know.

"Isn't this the most beautiful dress you've ever seen?"

Viewing her reflection in the mirror, she feels her entire body tingle, and her eyes begin to tear up. She's surprised that, with her petite size, the dress fits her perfectly.

"This is the perfect dress for my perfect day. I look like a bride."

Beth's happiness is infectious. Marie returns her infectious smile.

"Truthfully, this dress has been here for a while; it never looked like much on the rack, but on you I honestly believe it's the most beautiful dress I've ever seen in this shop."

Beth instantly feels this dress was created exclusively for her and only her.

"Well, let's see if Chloe agrees with us."

Beth is excited to show Chloe how the dress fits and exits the dressing room. She proceeds to the viewing area, surrounded by mirrors. With Marie's assistance, she steps onto the raised platform.

Before she turns to face Chloe, she catches her reflection in one of the many mirrors. Chloe's expression of awe reassures Beth of her choice. She appears stunned to see Beth in the elegant yet simple pink dress. It's the most stunning thing she's ever seen in her life.

"Beth, this dress was made for you. You were correct when you said you didn't want a white dress. Pink is the perfect choice and most definitely your color."

Beth smiles as she blushes but continues to admire the dress by twirling to make the feather-like wisps of fabric float.

Chloe notices the emotion building in Beth's eyes. She knows Beth is the perfect match for Marcus and can't wait to witness their beautiful life together. She jumps from her seat and hugs Beth.

"You're gorgeous. I think you found the perfect choice."

Fighting back tears that threaten to fall, Beth agrees.

"Yes, this is my dress. My wedding dress I will wear to marry Marcus."

With Beth's dress chosen, the pair focuses on finding a dress for Chloe. Chloe knows exactly what style and color look best on her. After only a couple of dress choices, she also finds a beautiful dress perfect for a beach wedding.

When both have completed their dress selections, Marie reminds Beth that they haven't chosen proper shoes.

"Do I need shoes for a beach wedding? I thought we agreed for both of us to be barefoot."

"Beth, you must wear shoes going to and from the ceremony location. So, I think you need to at least find something simple."

"See Chloe, this is why it was an excellent idea for you to assist me. I didn't think of much outside the ceremony on the beach."

She settles on a simple pair of white and gold slip-on sandals, while Chloe chooses a simple thong-style sandal. Beth is happy Chloe was included in her special day, only realizing today how much she misses female companionship.

With their purchases made, Chloe calls Bobby to let him know they've finalized their shopping and are ready to go to the heliport.

Bobby initially wants to make a joke about how long it took them, but he senses their happy tones and chooses only to say he's already outside waiting on them to exit.

With their prized purchases in hand, they are both smiling proudly when they arrive at the car, Beth begins to apologize for the time it took her to choose a dress. Bobby assures her today was her day to find the perfect dress, and she had no timeline. Chloe agrees, stating it was precisely what they had done.

"It was worth every minute we spent in there today; Beth bought the most beautiful wedding dress. Marcus will love it."

She hugs Beth, thanking her for allowing her to participate in this momentous event.

"One day, I'll be able to share with the world that I took part in Marcus Donovan's wedding to the love of his life."

"Yeah, one day."

Bobby loads the dresses and shoes into the back of the SUV while Beth and Chloe continue talking nonstop about their day together.

With a satisfied smile, Bobby realizes they have already become fast friends, quickly beginning a lifetime friendship, and he couldn't be happier.

CHAPTER TWENTY NINE

The three passengers, along with their prized possessions, arrive at the heliport to find Marcus and Mancuso already waiting in the helicopter. Smiles are exchanged as Bobby assists the ladies and their purchases aboard. Once everyone is safely inside, they are in the air for a short journey.

"Beth darling, we're now on our way to the island where we will vow to love each other forever," Marcus explained.

"This sounds like the easiest thing I can do for the rest of my life," Beth vowed.

As promised, the flight is short. Upon arriving, they find two cars and drivers waiting to take them to the secluded private hotel, all arranged by Bobby.

Beth is amazed and wonders how Bobby arranged to have a hotel exclusively for them, on a days' notice at that.

Before Beth has the opportunity to ask, Marcus begins.

"Do I even want to know 'how' you reserved and entire hotel?"

"Boss you know money talks—and your money speaks volumes. Nothing but the best for you and your beautiful bride."

"I won't ask any more questions, as I assume they were booked before your call."

"Humm, I didn't ask. I just threw out a number and asked if we could reserve the hotel, they responded immediately it was yours. Maybe they got a bad review or something. Or maybe they have bugs."

"Stop dude! You are incorrigible."

"You asked for a honeymoon suite, I got you a honeymoon hotel. Make sure Mancuso knows I get the gold star today, OK?"

"You did excellent, thanks. It is beautiful."

When they enter the hotel, Marcus receives an envelope with details about the wedding planning schedule for tomorrow. The agenda is broken down to the minute. A breakfast, lunch and dinner menu is listed, along with an inquiry about any special requests or restrictions they have.

The officiant plans to meet with them before lunch to finalize ceremony details, discuss the beach location, review documents, and sign them.

Marcus's heart skips a beat as he tries to imagine how beautiful Beth will be when he promises to love her forever, with the ocean consuming the sun behind them.

He hears low giggles between Beth and Chloe, and when he looks, sees them smiling and whispering among themselves.

"Am I to guess everything went well at the boutique, and your happy chatter means you're pleased and excited with your purchases?" Marcus asks.

"You can't even imagine how beautiful your bride will be tomorrow. Her dress choice is perfect," Chloe responds.

"I have no doubt she'll be the most beautiful bride ever. But now I'm even more excited to see her in this perfect dress you speak of," Marcus says.

***

The next morning, the group completes all the morning agenda items without incident. They also finalize all the necessary documents to get married. Next, they view a couple of beach locations and instantly know when they find the perfect one. Of course, they choose to be married at the water's edge, barefoot, with the water softly lapping at their feet at sunset.

Midafternoon, Marcus and Beth share a final hug and a quick kiss as they say,

"Love you. See you soon. Meet you at sunset."

Bobby and Chloe then whisk each of them away to their designated rooms to prepare for their dream ceremony in the sand.

***

Chloe pampers Beth by applying her makeup and styling her hair.

"All brides should be pampered on their wedding day, no exceptions. Thank you for allowing me to share this day with you."

When Chloe finally allows Beth to see her reflection, she doesn't even recognize the woman staring back at her. She sees a happy, stunning woman with true love showing in her eyes, a person she hasn't seen in a long while. Beth smiles as she praises Chloe for making her look gorgeous on her wedding day.

"Doll you are already beautiful; I only enhanced what you already have," Chloe replies.

Chloe opens a bottle of wine—aka grape juice—and produces a box of chocolates.

"Every bride deserves 'wine' and chocolate as she waits for her prince charming."

It's true; Beth feels like a princess. She has never experienced the pampering that Chloe is showing her today.

"Thank you Chloe. I'll never forget this day or all you've done for me. You've gone above and beyond to make this an incredible, lasting memory for me."

"When you marry Marcus, you'll be family. I'm happy to welcome you to our family. You make Marcus happy. We should thank you for loving him and bringing joy back to his life of chaos."

They chat as they sit together, drinking faux wine and patiently waiting for the time Beth will put on her beautiful dress. It has been hanging in view all afternoon, and Beth still marvels at its beauty each time she glances at it. As she sits, drinking the fake wine, she takes the time to study the dress in detail. It is truly breathtaking, and she hopes Marcus will share the same sentiment. Chloe seems to read her thoughts.

"He'll be mesmerized, I promise you."

"The dress is perfect. Isn't it."

"Yes and you will look amazing and perfect wearing it."

***

Yesterday, Marcus and Mancuso flew to purchase his wedding attire. He knew his outfit had to be perfect when he married his beautiful bride.

Most men would don a suit and call it a day. Not Marcus; he's known for his sense of fashion. He wants to match Beth's energy, recalling their first encounter when he noted her surprisingly unconventional style.

The only details about the attire they discussed beforehand was that they'd both be barefoot, getting married at the water's edge at sunset.

Wanting to look perfect for her, he decided on a two-piece cool white linen outfit. He now hopes it wasn't a mistake to choose white. His initial reasoning was that white symbolized new beginnings for them both. Now, he worries whether their attire will blend too much together or, conversely, portray them as a unified couple, which was his intention when he made the choice. Will Beth feel he's stealing her spotlight as the bride if they both wear white?

Now worried, he asks Bobby to check in with Chloe, getting her opinion about his choice of white without alerting Beth. After all, he did buy another outfit he could wear, a Plan B. Yet his first choice is the white one. He smiles, remembering how a Plan B outfit brought them to where they are today.

Chloe gives Bobby a thumbs-up when he asks, saying she thinks they'll look beautiful in their attire choices. She imagines how stunning they'll both be against the setting sun.

Marcus is relieved when Bobby returns with Chloe's approval. He's still nervous but not about marrying Beth or the ceremony. He's worried about her being consumed by his career and his chaotic life of stardom. He vows here and now to do everything possible to prevent this from happening.

***

The time has come for Marcus and Bobby to leave the hotel. When they arrive, they find the officiant already there, waiting patiently. Before walking toward the water's edge, Marcus takes a moment to revel in the moment. The spot they chose is beautiful.

As he looks out to the ocean, he's overcome with emotion. In a short time, his life will change forever, and he can hardly wait. For a moment, he thinks of his parents and wishes they could attend. He knows it's impossible right now, as they're being stalked relentlessly during their travels in hopes of locating him.

Bobby notices his friend is lost in his thoughts and emotions.

"Hey, buddy, it's not too late to cut and run, you know."

"Nah, it's not like that. I'm not second-guessing my marriage to Beth. I was just thinking of my parents and how I wish things were different."

"Max and Jo will understand. Besides, you always have me. I can't seem to get rid of you, so there's that."

"Nope my friend, you are stuck with me."

"Glad to know. Cause I'm not going anywhere."

"Now, let's go get in place for the arrival of your beautiful bride."

Minutes later, Mancuso arrives with Beth and Chloe. Marcus watches as they exit the car. Even with them still quite a ways up the beach, he sees how breathtaking she is, with her beauty and elegance. He then notices Mancuso extend his arm and begin escorting Beth toward him. He really is her fill-in dad, and he is overjoyed about it.

Speechless and emotional from the scene he's witnessing, he almost forgets his plan to sing to her as she approaches him.

He begins gently singing a newly written song about love and happiness. Beth feels her heart melting. She's being serenaded down the aisle by the love of her life, the father of her baby. Marcus Donovan loves her, and he's beckoning her toward him with his song of love.

As she steps beside him, it's only then that he realizes her dress is pink and the most magnificent piece of work he's ever seen. No one would ever guess it wasn't designed especially for her. It fit her perfectly.

Marcus quietly whispers, "You take my breath away a little more every time I see you. You're beautiful my love. I'll be proud to have you by my side for the rest of my life."

Bobby and Chloe both marvel at the beautiful couple standing before them, on the ocean's edge, with gentle waves lapping their bare feet.

Beth had asked Chloe to take a few photos after the ceremony. She had no idea Chloe also decided to take pictures during their vows. Bobby, without being asked, decides to video their commitment ceremony to share their lives.

Marcus and Beth each say their own vows, which leave the small group's hearts bursting with love and hope for the future of this powerful couple. There isn't a dry eye in attendance; even the officiant has a glimmer in his eye when all is said and done. He continues with longevity prayers before pronouncing them husband and wife.

As he says, "You may kiss the bride," Marcus already has Beth in his arms and dips her back toward the setting sun as he kisses his new wife. This action creates a vision only seen in magazines after many attempts to get it perfect.

Yet, unaware of anything or anyone but each other, they create the most breathtaking moment imaginable.

Chloe is sure she's gotten the stunning shot! She's thankful for setting her camera to burst shots, ensuring she missed nothing. She looks to Bobby and finds he's still recording. She can see in his expression, the happiness he feels for his dear friend.

Marcus looks at Bobby with such pride and love as he waves them all to come over and take a few photos with them before the sun disappears into the night.

The self-made family of five has five minutes, taking as many photos as possible before the sun is enveloped by the ocean. Chloe doesn't mention the million-dollar shot or any other pictures she took during the ceremony. She quickly decides a framed photo would make an excellent surprise wedding gift for them.

***

After taking as many photos as the sun permits, the group returns to the hotel. They sign the final dotted line and legally become Mr. and Mrs. Donovan.

Bobby arranged for the hotel to prepare a special dinner, and the five of them chat excitedly about the rapid change of events over the last week and the unexpected, beautiful outcome.

Marcus is unable to take his eyes off his wife in her perfect dress. He can't wait to hear how she chose a pink dress, as seeing her in it, he cannot visualize her in anything else.

He knows once again, his friends have, without hesitation, assisted him in areas he couldn't navigate by himself.

"I want each of you to know how important you are in our lives. Without you and your love and support, today couldn't have happened as flawlessly as it did. You're not just our friends; you're our family. We love you all dearly."

"Boss man we wouldn't have wanted to be anywhere else but here, sharing your dream. We thank you for including us," Bobby replies.

Mancuso raises a glass. "Congratulations to an amazing couple. May you both have many years of happiness. Marcus, you are welcome for allowing me to introduce Beth to your world. I remind you of the promise you made to always protect our girl. Cheers."

They all toast the happy couple, with grape juice, of course.

"I know it's still early, but we've had a few long and eventful days. Now it's time to get my blushing bride to bed. Please excuse us; we'll see you all in the morning."

He smiles as he says it, and Beth is sure she sees him exchange a wink with Bobby. Bobby has become familiar with

Marcus's look when he talks about Beth; he understands and winks back at his friend.

"Make sure you sleep well boss. I know how exhausted you are and all."

"Chloe, how do you ... I mean really... he is a mess, all the time."

"I can still hear you, goodnight boss."

With everyone laughing and Beth blushing, the newlyweds, Mr. and Mrs. Donovan, say their final goodnights as they leave to adjourn to their honeymoon suite.

Once inside their room, Beth becomes unusually quiet. Marcus takes her in his arms and gently asks her to share her thoughts. He sees the undeniable love in her eyes as she raises them to him. Her voice quivers slightly.

"This life I have with you, here and now, is unbelievable. If I'm dreaming, please don't wake me."

"What's unbelievable is that I never imagined you and your love existed out in this huge world. However, we found each other. I love you Beth Donovan. If this is a dream, I also beg never to wake up."

He seals his words with a kiss. Again, as with all the other times, the kiss explodes into a night of magical lovemaking, better than the times before for both.

As they lie in each other's arms, breathless and content, Beth snuggles into Marcus's neck and whispers, "Good night Mr. Donovan."

To which he replies, "Good night Mrs. Donovan."

They both then drift off into a sweet and satisfied slumber.

CHAPTER THIRTY

Marcus wakes up to find the bed empty. Momentarily, he wonders if yesterday was a dream. Then his eyes settle on Beth seated at a small desk, writing in a book. He quietly watches her, trying to decide if she's writing in a journal. He can tell by the dampness of her hair that she's already showered and dressed. His heart sinks for a second, as he was hoping for a repeat of last night's wedding night consummation.

Placing his focus back on Beth, he thinks whatever she's writing must be important.

When he speaks, his voice is husky with desire.

"Good morning my beautiful bride."

She looks up from her writing, and as she raises her eyes to meet his, she sees his undeniable love.

"Good morning to you my dear husband."

She rises and crosses the room to the bed. She tries to sound casual as she asks, "I trust you slept well as a married man."

"Yes ma'am, my wife is the perfect bedmate. My only complaint is that she wasn't beside me when I woke up."

"Exactly how many bedmates are you comparing your wife to?"

Marcus doesn't miss a beat with his reply.

"Not as many as rumored."

"Good to know."

She sits beside him and leans in, giving him a proper good morning kiss. No surprise to either of them, the intensity increases immediately.

Beth pretends to protest, saying she's already showered and dressed. Marcus assures her he'll gladly assist her with a repeat shower, but adds it might take a while for the latter to happen. Beth is once again overwhelmed with emotion at the thought of the effect she has on him and he on her. Her body always betrays her; she becomes feverish to share her love with him.

Once Beth has showered and dressed for the second time, they leave the room to join Mancuso, Bobby, and Chloe in the dining area. Beth knows she's foolish, but she blushes, knowing their damp hair is a dead giveaway of their morning activities. She's still modest; even though they're married and she's pregnant, she likes to keep their intimacy private.

Beth smiles as they exchange morning greetings, trying to sound casual.

"I trust everyone had a good night's rest. I'll jump right to the point. I have plenty to discuss if it's okay with everyone."

She pulls out the notebook Marcus saw her writing in earlier when he awoke.

The four exchange glances of slight confusion, but as Beth starts talking, none of the men are surprised by her take-charge manner or to hear she's created a plan. Beth always has a plan; they're now just curious about what she's going to say.

Chloe however, looks shocked and is the first to speak. "Beth can't business wait? You're on your honeymoon, you know."

Both Bobby and Mancuso shake their heads toward Chloe.

"No use Chloe; Beth always has a plan, so we might as well hear what she has on her mind so we can have time to visit the beach before we leave," Bobby says.

Beth should have taken offense to these words, but she doesn't. She knows Bobby isn't being rude, only factual. She also knows he trusts that it must be important if she has something to plan.

"Sorry, yes, we're here on our honeymoon, but I need to propose this idea before we head back home. I started compiling a plan when I found out I was pregnant, but the last three days happened so fast that I never finalized my thoughts until this morning."

Marcus, who has been quietly listening, engages her with spiked curiosity.

"I thought you were writing in a journal this morning; you were deciding on a plan? What did I miss, and what kind of plan are we making? Why do we need a plan?"

"It's not a plan; it's an idea. I have an idea I'd love to share."

"So, what kind of idea?"

Beth takes a deep breath, hoping Marcus understands and doesn't misconstrue her intention. For an instant, she gets nervous about his reaction. But she knows if he listens openly, he'll agree to the possibility of it working seamlessly.

"So, we all know how much Marcus desires his private life to remain private."

She looks directly into his eyes, and he nods in agreement.

"No secret there, you all know my situation."

"Let me preface by saying that I love that I'm now Mrs. Marcus Donovan, and you know I'd love nothing more than to shout it from the mountaintops. However, we both know you'll never get a moment's peace once the world knows about me and the baby."

She sees the hurt and confusion on his face, and it breaks her heart. She also notices that he recognizes the reality of this.

"I have an idea, one allowing us to live together in plain sight without anyone knowing about our true relationship."

Now, they're all curious. Marcus is the first to speak up. "Please continue, as this sounds next to impossible."

Beth slightly relaxes when she realizes she has his attention, and his interest is sparked.

"So, Marcus Allen Donovan, I'll stay employed as your personal assistant and security detail when you decide to return to your life in the real world. I'll attend all your events, concerts, shows, etc., as Beth Allen, wife of Donnie Allen. Do you see what I did?"

She waits for a second, but no one objects, so she continues with her idea.

"We'll live in the real world as Mr. and Mrs. Donnie Allen. You'll live under an alias. We'll be able to fly under the media's radar. As I said, we'll live together in plain sight. When we move to the ranch, these will be our names. Until then, I'll be Beth Allen, married to Donnie."

Bobby smiles as he listens to Beth explain and thinks, *Of course, you have a plan; you always do.* He remembers their first encounter and how impressed he was with her planning.

He also knows if they disagree with this plan, there's a backup plan, a Plan B.

Chloe sits listening, impressed to watch Beth present her idea to the group. Bobby had told her about Beth's take-charge attitude and planning strategies, which had impressed him from the start. But to be sitting here and watching her in action is amazing.

Chloe is the first to respond. She claps her hands and begins speaking because she completely understands what Beth is proposing.

"Wow, this is an excellent idea Beth! Oh my gosh, Bobby said you were always two steps ahead of everyone in the room. I don't have a vote, but I think you both might be able to pull this off."

Chloe smiles, thinking Beth really is the perfect match for Marcus.

Beth glances between Bobby, Mancuso, and Marcus. None look fully invested in the idea, but at least Bobby is smiling.

"The decision doesn't need to be made today or tomorrow. If we stay on the island, there'll be no rush. The thought of our marriage complicating things in the media for Marcus causes me sadness. Everyone here knows I always try to have a plan to ease a complication."

She looks directly at Marcus, staring him in the eyes.

"I love you Marcus, and I'm incredibly proud to be Mrs. Donovan. I'll gladly call the paparazzi and tell them myself if you want me to. I'll tell anyone and everyone who'll listen that you're the love of my life."

Marcus places his hand on hers.

"I know babe, and you're correct in everything. I just hadn't thought past us today, and not our future. I should have, but I never gave thought to the media and didn't try to plan our future in the real world. I'm sorry."

Beth leans over and places a light kiss on his cheek.

"There's no need to apologize. We're a team, and I'll always have ideas to discuss with you."

Bobby, who has remained silent, not uttering a single word, speaks up.

"Well, we've laid a foundation for an alias identity. Of course, we must develop a clear and solid concept, but personally, I think this can work."

They agree to table the conversation until they get home. Today, they'll enjoy exploring this beautiful island, and tomorrow, the helicopter returns to take them back to their island, back home.

At dinner, Marcus invites Chloe to spend a couple of days at the Triple M. She's excited to spend more time with her husband and get a glimpse into the world they've created on this tiny island she's heard so much about. She's also happy to spend more time with Beth, as they've become fast friends. She gladly accepts his invitation.

CHAPTER THIRTY ONE

Returning home to their private oasis, everyone decides to wait a few days before continuing their discussion about Beth's idea of an alias. No one has verbally rejected the idea, and there was no further discussion during their stay at the hotel.

Two days after the small group of five returns to the Triple M, Bobby and Chloe approach John in the security house, asking for his assistance. They ask him to print and save the wedding photos and video.

They've managed to keep them a secret from the newlyweds and would love to surprise them before leaving in a few days.

John is excited to participate in another part of the Donovan wedding. He agrees to have it completed before he leaves the day after tomorrow. Chloe asks if there's any way he could print the 'million-dollar' shot. He agrees to contact Jackson and have him send large photo paper and a picture frame. He can't wait to share with Jackson all that has transpired in the week he's been gone.

John hands off the larger printing supply request to Jackson, assuring Chloe she'll get her requested print. Meanwhile,

Chloe and John compile a small photo album of the ceremony photos.

When New Beginnings arrives with a special delivery, he is able to then print and frame the breathtaking 'kiss the bride' photo. All videos are secure on a flash drive, as well as backed up on the security house hard drive.

***

Bobby and Chloe surprise Marcus and Beth with the photo album and flash drive of the ceremony video. They're both speechless and grateful for their forethought to create this unexpected and amazing gift for them.

They were aware photos were taken after the ceremony with the sunset, but both were shocked to receive the actual ceremony photos. The video Bobby took is irreplaceable; they cannot thank him enough. He was very thoughtful to think to capture this memory for them,

When they're presented with a larger print of the "kiss the bride" photo, they all agree it's the most breathtaking photo they've ever seen. Beth has no words, as tears form in the corners of her eyes.

Marcus promises Beth he'll have this fantastic picture transferred to a canvas and hung in both Las Vegas and Oklahoma.

While the friends are still gathered together, Marcus proudly announces he'd like to share some news.

He takes Beth's hand and continues, "I thought tonight would be the perfect time to announce I've named the island. Call it a wedding gift of sorts to my new bride."

Chloe is once again the first to be excited as she asks, "Well, how long are you going to make us wait? The anticipation is killing me."

"I'm getting there. Just let me say why I chose the name first. The description is powerfully and mysteriously attractive."

"The name of our island is Allure."

Beth squeezes his hand as her eyes glisten, daring the tears to fall. "The name is perfect, my love."

"The name wasn't only chosen for the island, but also for you darling."

Bobby, true to his nature, blurts out, "Yeah, yeah. We get it. You're in love. Mushy-mushy. Kissy-kissy. Please, can we talk about something else, anything else, like maybe this whole alias thing?"

Marcus laughs once again at his friend.

"Well, I've thought about it, nonstop actually. I say let's try this. I'll do anything to keep Beth and our baby safe. Who knows, it could work. We won't know until we try."

"Well, it sounds like the Allens are going to be established. What're your thoughts Mancuso?"

Mancuso, who has been quiet the entire night, now speaks up with his opinion.

"I too, have given this much thought. I agree with Marcus; let's try. With our connections, we have the ability to create this identity."

For the next few hours, the group of friends, who are family, discuss how they will go about securing everything needed for the Allens to exist.

***

Tonight is Chloe's last night on the island. Tomorrow, she and Bobby will return home to Oklahoma. She and Beth discuss the unbelievable week they've had and what life will look like when Beth and Marcus move to the ranch under their new aliases. They laugh and giggle at the thought of Marcus Donovan living right under people's noses, all while they're unaware of his identity.

"Just think Marcus Donovan living as Donnie Allen on a ranch in Oklahoma. Living in plain sight."

The following day, Beth hugs Chloe and begs her to return to visit soon. Chloe agrees, hoping to see them at least one more time before the baby arrives, saying she'll most definitely be back after the arrival of their bundle of joy. Beth watches as Chloe and Bobby board *New Beginnings* and head back to the reality of the mainland.

Marcus and Beth then head back toward the Triple M, hand in hand.

"Alone at last, Mrs. Donovan," Marcus announces once they step inside the massive door.

"Oh my, what must we do now, Mr. Donovan?"

As if on cue, the door swings open, and Rosie, the chef, and Mancuso join them in the room.

They smile at each other as they go to Marcus's office, resuming their daily routine. Except today they are focused on discussing details on the alias, Donnie Allen. Before long, Donnie is quickly beginning to take on an unexpected reality.

With most of the key elements decided, they realize they need documents to support this new identity. Mere days later, when Mancuso puts the necessary documents in their possession, they decide it's best not to ask *how* he managed to obtain them.

***

Marcus is excited for their first opportunity to use the new alias. His first mission is that they need to find a personal midwife for Beth. They need to hire someone who will come to the island and agree to stay with them when the delivery is close.

They discuss the option of having someone who can provide prenatal care after her initial visit to an obstetrician, ensuring both are healthy enough to proceed with a personal midwife.

Beth agrees, except she tells Marcus she wants to see Dr. Scott for her initial visit. She trusts him. He was a gentle and sincere man, and they wouldn't have to add another person into their private lives. Even though he's currently in family medicine, he did tell her he was formerly an OB doctor. Marcus trusts Beth's instincts.

***

Beth schedules and attends an initial appointment with Dr. Scott. He does her pregnancy exam and extensive lab work, giving her a clean bill of health. He's surprised to notice her last name is now "Allen" and congratulates her on her nuptials.

"I assume this means the father was happy with the news."

"Yes, he was very pleased."

Then she requests information about a personal midwife, and if he had any recommendations, Dr. Scott beams. He instantly knows the perfect choice for her. He scribbles down a name and number on a prescription pad and hands it to Beth.

"Katie is the best. You'll be delighted to have her during your pregnancy and the birthing process."

Beth contacts Katie as soon as she leaves Dr. Scott's office, hoping to meet with her while she's still on the mainland. Katie answers the phone in a friendly tone and she agrees to meet Beth, giving her the address to her home.

Katie, a mature woman with a warm smile, she reminds Beth of Dr. Scott. She's very patient and understanding with Beth's many questions and concerns.

During this first encounter, Katie asks if the father will be attending any visits and the birth. Beth has to think fast, as she hasn't anticipated this question so soon.

"Of course, I know Donnie wants to be here, but honestly, I'm unsure. You see, he travels a lot for work. Our current plan is for him to attend the birth. Our situation is complicated. His career demands travel, and I'm currently on assignment here."

She feels guilty; this alias thing might be more complicated than she anticipated. Oh well, she has started it now, so she continues.

"Thankfully, my boss is very understanding and allows me to remain here during my pregnancy and birth. He doesn't want me to be alone if Donnie can't return in time."

Her quick on the fly response satisfies Katie.

As the months pass, Katie never again asks about the father, Donnie.

CHAPTER THIRTY TWO

Thankfully, the morning sickness has subsided and seems to be in the past. Beth is excited about the baby, but truthfully, she's glad that unappealing part of the pregnancy is over.

Her baby bump has made its presence known, and Marcus constantly rubs her belly and sings to their growing child. Katie has been keeping a close eye on her with monthly visits, each time giving her a positive growth report.

Beth and Marcus continue their nightly walks to *Sunset Beach.* The beauty they witness never gets old. Tonight, as they sit in silence, Beth feels tiny bubbles fluttering in her belly.

"Oh my! Babe, I'm not sure, but I think our baby just gave their approval of the beautiful sight we just witnessed."

Marcus instantly moves his hand to her baby bump, hoping to feel the flutters. Beth giggles.

"Silly, I could barely feel it, so you are not able to, yet. But soon this little one will be active all the time."

***

When Beth is six months pregnant, Marcus suggests that she should sell her townhouse, as her new life no longer includes returning to North Carolina. Beth agrees and contacts her realtor for an appointment.

She makes the trip to NC without incident as she has multiple times.

Her meeting with the realtor is promising, and they anticipate the townhome will sell quickly due to its high-demand location. They complete the paperwork for a potential sale, as the realtor already has someone in mind. Beth pre-signs the necessary legal closing documents. Her townhome sale seems much clearer cut, than when she sold her house.

Beth decides to take a day and visit Mike and Carol, her former neighbors, one afternoon after arranging for her townhome furnishings to be moved to her storage unit. She'll decide what to do with the unit's contents after the baby arrives.

Mike and Carol are excited to see Beth and shocked to discover she has got married and is now pregnant since they last saw her. Naturally, they ask for all the details.

Beth feels guilty about telling them the made-up story of Donnie Allen, but she has no choice. She hopes she can share the truth with them one day and prays they'll understand her need for secrecy. After a lengthy visit, as Beth prepares to leave, she finds herself dizzy, almost passing out when she stands up.

Mike helps her back to the couch. Carol, concerned when she notices that the color has drained from Beth's face, convinces her they should call 911. Beth hesitantly agrees, but only because she knows she shouldn't drive feeling like this and also for the baby's sake. She tries to stand again, but everything spins, so she retreats back to the couch and waits for emergency assistance.

When the ambulance arrive, they review her vitals and advise her that her blood pressure is extremely low, they recommend transport to the hospital for a complete workup due to her current stage of pregnancy.

Once she arrives at the hospital, they run tests and blood work, monitoring her vital signs closely. The doctor unsure of the cause of her symptoms, orders an overnight stay for observation.

Beth needs to call Marcus, but she is afraid she will break down and sound weak, She doesn't want to upset him.

Instead, she gathers her courage and tries not to sound anxious when she calls Bobby. She updates him about the reason she won't be arriving home tonight as planned. Beth tells him she is optimistic that everything will be fine overnight, and she'll come home tomorrow.

She ends the call with a final request, "Please do not let Marcus worry, the baby and I will be fine."

Home, she thinks. Her townhome is empty, and although she still owns it, it's no longer home. The island is home. Marcus is home.

***

The next morning, when the doctor visits, he shares his concerns about discharging her, as he knows she plans to board a plane. He is worried for her to travel alone.

As if on cue, Bobby comes waltzing through the door as the doctor is reviewing her test results and any possible complications with her.

"Hi sis. I got here as quickly as I could. I'm here to make sure you get home safely."

Beth smiles at him, thinking that the lie he told came all too easily for him.

"Bobby, I told you I'd be fine. The doctor is reviewing all the concerns and results now, as well as my discharge instructions."

"Well, you know how Donnie gets when he's not available. He made me promise to drop everything and get you home safely. I even brought Katie with me."

The doctor seems to relax, knowing Beth won't be alone on her travel home. "Who's Katie?"

Once they inform him that Katie is her midwife, the discharge proceeds smoothly and quickly. Only when they're in the privacy of the car does Beth begin to question his true motive.

"Bobby, why are you really here?"

"I told you, Marcus insisted I come and get you. Let's get moving; the jet is waiting. By the way, I told the doctor the truth—Katie is waiting for you on board."

All Beth could think is, *Wow Marcus must be distraught if he sent Bobby, the jet and Katie too.* She doesn't say this out loud.

"All this for a little dehydration, but I feel fine now. Please call Marcus right now so he won't continue to worry about me."

Bobby nods as they navigate traffic to the private area of the airfield. She hears muffled tones as Bobby speaks on the phone, but not the actual conversation.

Once on the plane, Katie meets Beth at the door, hovering over her like a mother hen. Beth smiles as she lets Katie fuss over her.

Within minutes of boarding, the pilot instructs them to take their seats and prepare for takeoff. The flight will take two hours.

Fifteen minutes into the flight, Bobby asks Beth to go into the private quarters and retrieve a document he needs to review for Donnie.

When she opens the door and steps inside, she sees Marcus leaning on the desk, his brow furrowed with concern and his face showing worry for her.

She crosses the room, needing to touch him, to be embraced by him. Once in his arms, she feels the entire weight of the stress and fear of the last couple of days. It is rapidly catching up with her.

She feels safe as she allows herself to cry softly as he holds her in his arms. Through her tears, she reassures him that both she and the baby are fine, and she's crying because she's happy to see him. She needs him; he's her safety.

***

Once they're back home on the island, Marcus hovers over Beth's every move. He monitors her meals, constantly reminding her to eat and drink in proper amounts. Beth knows he's doing this because of his love for her, so she doesn't protest much.

Marcus arranges for Katie to come daily, saying it's just for now to ensure Beth has no further issues. He tries not to be overprotective, but he fails daily, making her love him that much more.

***

A month after returning home from North Carolina, Marcus begs Beth to return to his mansion in Las Vegas. She wants to disagree, but she knows Marcus is concerned about her and the baby. He was scared when the incident happened in NC and they were not together. He fled his famous life, choosing isolation over a year ago, and now he's willing to return for their safety.

He also offers for Katie to join them, to which she agrees. Mancuso will also be making the trip with them.

Their private jet returns to Las Vegas in the early morning hours. The trip is uneventful, and Beth sleeps for a few hours. Still unaware of their marital status, having Katie with them makes it impossible for Beth to have Marcus hold her while she sleeps.

They arrive to find Bobby waiting for them at the airstrip. Marcus requested the limo so Beth could have more comfort than the SUV.

Due to the time, their arrival at the mansion occurs unnoticed by the paparazzi, which pleases the small group. The longer Marcus's return remains unknown, the better.

CHAPTER THIRTY THREE

They had been at the mansion for a couple of weeks when Marcus told Beth he had received notice that his parents were back in the States. He also let her know that he had invited them for a visit. They were excited to hear from their son and even more so to see him.

Marcus hadn't abandoned his parents when he went into isolation. He was a good son. He stayed in touch with his parents via postcards. Marcus had friends from around the world forward his postcards to them. Recently, he had let them know he would be returning home to Las Vegas soon. However, they had no idea about Beth or the baby. This was not the kind of information one wrote on a postcard.

He was excited to introduce his mom and dad to his new wife. He was positive they would love her as much as he did. He could not wait to see his mom's reaction when she learned she would soon be a grandmother. Smiling, he remembered his loving childhood and knew his parents would treat his wife and child with the same tender love.

Beth was anxious to meet Marcus's parents. He had assured her they would love her, and she hoped it was true. After all, she did marry their son, and they were not invited. She prayed they would forgive her, understanding it was planned in two days.

***

When Max and Jo Donovan arrived at the mansion, Marcus met them at the door. His mom, Jo, hugged him tightly as if she were afraid to let go, fearing he was just a dream. Her eyes teared up. She had missed her isolated son this past year. This was the longest time they had ever been out of direct contact.

His dad, Max, smiled widely, instantly noticing this was the most relaxed and happy he had seen his son in a long time. His eyes glistened as he beamed with love.

"Come on now Jo, let our boy breathe."

His mother reluctantly released him; Max then extended his right hand to shake his son's hand. Marcus pulled him in, hugging him tightly.

"Good to see you son. We have missed you."

Marcus, not knowing where to begin explaining about Beth, who was waiting for them in the next room, decided to jump right to the point.

"Mom, Dad, I met someone. I know you will love her as much as I do. I am so sorry I have not told you about her before now, but I couldn't risk any breach in our communication.

Therefore, I had no choice but to wait and tell you about her face to face."

Max and Jo saw the mixture of heartbreak and joy in his announcement. They both reassured him, saying they understood his silence and solitude over the past year. They commented that they were thankful to see his time away had served its purpose; he appeared relaxed and happy.

"Don't worry son. You did what you had to do. We are just glad to see you found happiness. We both thought you looked different in the photo you sent, happier."

Marcus smiled brightly at their words.

"I am happy. Mom, Dad, her name is Beth, and I cannot wait for you both to meet her. Not only is she perfect, but she is also perfect for me."

Max and Jo smiled and said they were excited to meet this woman who had stolen their son's heart and made him so happy.

He began cautiously, making sure to choose the right words. This was the first time he had ever been able to introduce Beth as his wife, and he wanted to get it right.

"There's something else. Before I take you to meet her… we got married, and… we are having a baby."

He searched both of his parents' faces for disappointment or shock but saw only joy and excitement. His mom was crying.

Before he could process their reactions, she had once again hugged him so tightly he could barely breathe. Squeezing him tighter than before, she gave a high squeal and began bouncing up and down.

"Oh son! I am so happy. It's about time you found true love and a life partner. I am going to be a grandmother. Oh my, I never expected to hear this. I am so happy."

She squeezed him again, asking excitedly when they could meet their new daughter-in-law.

Marcus was elated. His parents were excited, and they didn't blame him for not informing them of his nuptials when they occurred.

"She is waiting in the private living room. You can meet her now. There is a great deal we must update you about—a lot to discuss. Mom, I am genuinely sorry that our only correspondence has been so general, and I couldn't share this with you before."

Jo nodded. She was sad but also knew he was correct in keeping this life-changing information out of print.

His friends from around the world had been sending them postcards from him. Still, the generic postcards she received somehow got leaked to the media. The variety of postmarks had sent everyone searching for her son at locations worldwide.

Max remained calm as he processed the happy yet unexpected news.

"Well son, we have waited a long time for this day. How much longer before you let us meet our new daughter-in-law?"

"Dad, you will love her, I promise. Let's go meet Beth. She is nervous, which I find funny since not much rattles her. She is usually confident and sure. I find it cute to see her off her game."

He smiled at them, leading them to the private living room.

***

Beth stood with her back to the door, looking out the window. She heard their footsteps as they entered.

"Babe my parents are here."

Beth heard the nervousness in Marcus's voice, making her smile as she turned to meet her new in-laws. She knew instantly by their shocked expressions that Marcus had omitted how far along she was in her pregnancy.

She crossed the room to greet them properly; however, Marcus's mom rushed to embrace her tightly.

"Oh my goodness, aren't you just the cutest thing I have ever seen!"

Once released from the unexpected but welcoming hug, she began to apologize.

"I am so sorry. I am so excited. Marcus said you were expecting, but of course he forgot to mention how soon. So, how long before I'm a grandma? Do we know if it's a boy or a girl?"

Marcus interrupted, laughing at his mom.

"Mom, Dad, this is my wife Beth. Beth, these are my overly excited, never-meet-a-stranger parents, Max and Jo."

Beth smiled, greeting them both warmly, assuring them their excitement made her happy.

Max took Beth's hand as he attempted to explain their behavior.

"I'm sorry if we seem to be too much; we are still absorbing everything Marcus told us. We are very surprised and even more excited. Would it be OK for me to hug you and welcome you to our family?"

Beth nodded, and the sweet man put his arms around her, hugging her tightly. Barely audible, she heard him whisper,

"Thank you for loving our son."

His sincere words made Beth tear up with emotion.

"He is very special sir, and easy to love. I love him very much."

***

With introductions made, they all gathered in the comfy sitting area. Marcus began sharing with his parents the highlights of the events of the last year. He told them about Beth's standout interview and how smitten he was when she entered the room. He talked about going into isolation and how it had allowed him to relax and successfully write several songs he was anxious to release.

He became emotional as he told them how beautiful Beth looked in her pink wedding dress, promising they would see the video Bobby took of their perfect wedding.

Then, lastly, he shared his alias, Donnie Allen. He did not get the reaction he expected from them. His parents looked at each other and burst out laughing. They saw the confusion on his face as they laughed.

Max was the first to subside and shared the reason.

"When I was younger, a few of my friends nicknamed me Donnie. What irony."

Marcus was surprised, as he had never heard this story.

"My wife has more in common with my parents than I realized."

Next, Marcus talked about his isolation over the past year. He emphasized that he wanted his parents to be part of their lives. However, he still would not disclose his location—or that it was an island—as too much was at stake. The hurt could be seen, and Beth felt sad for them, but she knew it was for the best.

***

A light knock was heard on the wall. Looking up, they saw Bobby as he strolled casually into the room.

"I heard a rumor there was a beautiful woman in here."

Jo blushed as she smiled and greeted Bobby with a slight wave, followed by an air kiss.

Bobby joined the conversation.

"So, isn't Beth just perfect? I'm still not sure if Marcus deserves her, but they do make a striking-looking pair. The baby will be stunning."

The room burst out in laughter. Beth felt a slight blush rise in her cheeks.

"All right buddy, if you plan on being an honorary papa, you can't just love Beth—she is my wife, you know."

"Yeah, yeah. After almost twenty years, you don't give me much choice. Besides, Beth will let me be papa, won't you dear?"

"I sure will but remember we talked about this—you have to accept Marcus."

"Touche. I love you both. I just like to make Marcus wonder sometimes."

"I never wonder. You are stuck with me, my friend."

"Exactly."

"Anyway, who wants an update on the new ranch in Oklahoma?"

Beth sat back and smiled at the ease and transition of the conversation, silently thankful to be accepted as part of this fantastic family.

CHAPTER THIRTY FOUR

The next month passed with Max and Jo doting over their new daughter-in-law and expected grandchild. However, it was sometimes tricky, as Marcus had informed them that the midwife was unaware he was the absent father.

When Beth's delivery date was only a couple of weeks away, she was sleeping when a sharp pain woke her. She knew having false labor weeks before her due date was common, so she was not alarmed as she showered and dressed for the day.

She was making her way to the kitchen when another sharp pain hit—this one made her gasp. This contraction had her full attention, and she checked her watch, just in case this was the real deal.

Five minutes later, while in the living room, she once again felt the same intense pain. Trying to appear calm, she searched for Marcus, who she found relaxed and drinking coffee with his dad.

"Hey babe, today might be a special day—the day we meet our precious gift."

The look on his face showed both fear and excitement as he understood what she was saying.

"Does this mean I need to inform Katie?"

"Yep, I think so."

It was all she managed to say before another sharp contraction hit.

Mancuso was on-site this month. Marcus pressed his watch and tried to stay calm as he instructed him to locate the midwife.

"Tony, we need Katie. Find her now."

Marcus crossed the room to Beth, taking her in his arms, feeling helpless.

"We still never devised a plan on how I can be with you during delivery."

Beth felt sad for them both; she wanted Marcus with her, but she knew the fewer people who knew their situation, the better. Still, her initial instinct was to throw caution to the wind—but only for a brief second. She knew it wasn't an option; she had to be strong. She would be strong.

"I know, but I'll be OK. Katie knows what she's doing."

Katie arrived in the living room to find Marcus pacing and Beth sitting in an overstuffed chair, her hand on her belly.

"Have you timed them?"

Beth was happy to see Katie; she relaxed a little and responded,

"This last one was about three and a half minutes."

"This is great Beth! It looks like your little bundle has decided today is their birthday."

They both heard the deep breath Marcus took as he continued to pace the room.

Beth wanted Marcus to hold her hand and tell her everything would be OK, but they couldn't. As if reading their minds, Katie made a bold statement that shocked them both.

"It is none of my business Mr. Marcus, but please comfort your baby's mother—she needs your love and support right now."

Stunned, Marcus and Beth exchanged glances of shock and bewilderment as they heard her continue speaking.

"I might be getting older, but I'm not blind to true love. I know there is no way you both don't want to experience this birthing process together."

Marcus didn't deny her statement. Instead, he felt relieved, and now all his attention was focused on Beth. He crossed the room to her as another contraction came. He held her until it passed, and then, taking her hand, they followed Katie to the room they had previously designated as the labor and birthing room.

Max, who had been sitting quietly watching the love and excitement, almost forgot to notify Jo of their grandchild's impending arrival. He immediately rushed from the room to find his wife and share the news.

***

As her labor intensified, Marcus held her hand and spoke gentle words of love and encouragement between the kisses he continually placed on her head.

"You're doing excellent babe. I love you so much, and I'm so proud of your strength."

When the pains became intense, occurring back-to-back, Beth wondered how she could endure the rapid, sharp contractions for another minute. She then heard Katie announce it was time to push.

"You've done an excellent job, Ms. Beth. Now it's time to push this precious bundle out into this big world and into Mommy and Daddy's open arms."

Before long, Katie commanded one final push and proudly presented them with a healthy baby girl.

Elizabeth Mae Donovan entered the world with only a slight cry. She quickly quieted when Marcus instinctively began singing softly to her. Beth, tired, smiled in awe at this beautiful, tiny human they had created from their love for each other. She wondered what she had done to be so blessed to have this amazing man in her life.

CHAPTER THIRTY FIVE

Even though they had never left the mansion since arriving, the ever-watchful paparazzi began to speculate that Marcus was back in town. The activity of cars entering and exiting triggered rumors within their circle about his possible return.

Within days of Lizzie's arrival, Rodney convinced Marcus to perform at an awards show. He began his pitch by explaining that rumors were already circulating about Marcus being back, so they needed to publicly confirm it for his fans. Rodney was a smart agent and knew Marcus would likely agree, if he made the fans the focus—which is exactly what he did.

Marcus agrees to attend the show because his fans are special to him. He knew they had been worried about him while he was away, and he hated that they had been left in the dark. He made a mental note to publicly thank them after the show for their patience and loyalty during his absence.

When he agreed to perform, his only condition was that he wanted to sing one of his newly written, unreleased songs. It would be a live segment featuring Marcus Donovan—and the network didn't care if he read poetry; they were simply thrilled to have him. Booking Marcus after over a year of isolation would skyrocket ratings. They gladly accepted his performance choice, whether it was a new track or an older hit.

The day before the show, Marcus discovers he has also been nominated for an award. Rodney had conveniently "forgotten" to mention this detail before Marcus accepted the invitation.

Although Marcus rarely lost his temper with Rodney, he spoke firmly about the importance of full disclosure for future appearances. Rodney apologized, admitting that Marcus might not be entirely ready to return to the public eye.

Marcus assured him that his time away had given him a new perspective on life—he felt stronger, grounded, and ready to face the media with Beth by his side. He also reminded Rodney that he could always retreat to the island if things became overwhelming.

Beth was disappointed she couldn't attend the show but looked forward to watching her husband perform on national television. After all, she heard him sing every day, serenading their beautiful daughter.

As she watched the broadcast, Beth was mesmerized by his performance. The song was new to the audience but familiar to her—she had heard it countless times during its creation at the Triple M. Still, she had never heard the final version with the full track until tonight. Her heart swelled as she realized the song was about her. A tear of pure love slipped down her cheek.

"Ditto, my love. Ditto."

She found herself jumping up and down with joy when Marcus won the award for Best Single, a song he had released before his isolation. His acceptance speech was short but heartfelt. He paused several times as the cheers and applause filled the room. Yet no one cheered louder than Beth, watching proudly from home.

Beth was certain he was blushing beneath the stage makeup. It was clear that everyone was thrilled to see him back in the spotlight. His speech carried subtle undertones and personal references that only Beth and those closest to him would understand. He thanked his fans for their loyalty and promised them more music soon.

As always, he thanked his parents, who were seated in the audience. When the camera panned to them, Beth saw their faces glowing with pride. His mother, in particular, looked emotional—tears shimmered in her eyes as she watched her son touch the world with his voice.

Before the night ended, Rodney was flooded with requests for guest appearances. Talk shows, morning shows, and late-night hosts all wanted Marcus—some to perform, others to interview him about his year of isolation. He made it clear that discussing his time away was off-limits, and they agreed to those terms.

Marcus told Rodney he could schedule appearances, but he would have final approval over which shows to accept. He preferred programs with hosts who respected boundaries and focused on the music rather than his private life.

When the shows were confirmed, producers asked to include his parents, but Max and Jo refused to be interviewed. They were there only to support their son and were content to watch from the sidelines.

Beth was proud of Marcus for stepping back into the limelight. His fans were thrilled, and his new single—performed for the first time at the awards show—quickly climbed the charts. He was back in the headlines, and his popularity was soaring once again.

Everything seemed to be going smoothly, so Beth was surprised when Marcus suddenly announced he was ready to go home—to the island. She assumed he would want to stay longer and enjoy the renewed attention. When she asked why, his answer was simple.

"I can record at home. I don't need all this fanfare. I'm ready to get back to our life—you, me, and Lizzie. Donnie Allen is ready to go home with his wife."

When Lizzie was eight weeks old, her private pediatrician cleared them for travel. The next day, they boarded a plane and returned to the island—ready to resume their quiet life and establish a new routine with their daughter.

***

Back at the Triple M, Beth and Marcus turned their attention to finalizing the design for their new home on the Oklahoma ranch. They decided to use the same floor plan as the Triple M, with a few modifications. The biggest difference was the exterior, designed to blend in and attract less attention. The top floor would be removed, except for a small loft that Marcus would use as an office, since the ground-floor office and studio were being converted into bedrooms. Additional rooms were added for a Master suite and playroom.

They added a garage, as well as front and back porches. For his music, Marcus was pleased when they decided to build a barn-style studio on the property. Bobby continues to oversee construction and kept them updated through photos and videos.

Marcus felt refreshed to be home. Inspiration flowed freely as he wrote songs about love and happiness—Beth and Lizzie being his greatest muses.

Both Beth and Marcus treasured their quiet island life, enjoying parenthood and their peaceful routine. Each evening, they still took their walks to watch the sunset, always with Lizzie in tow. She seemed to have adjusted perfectly to the salty air, and they swore she smiled every time the sun dipped below the horizon as her parents shared a kiss.

Beth was surprised one Wednesday morning when *New Beginnings* arrived carrying unexpected guests—Marcus's parents. Marcus had arranged their visit as a surprise. Through multiple transfers between commercial and private transport, they remained unaware of the island's exact location, respecting their son's need for secrecy.

Beth's former bedroom had been converted into a guest suite. Max and Jo found both the island and the house delightful. They enjoyed every minute spent with Lizzie—and with Beth and Marcus, of course. Nothing made them happier than watching their son thrive as a husband and father.

Beth was also thoroughly enjoying their visit. She loved hearing stories from Max and Jo as they compared Lizzie's features and personality to Marcus's childhood days.

***

Before long, Rodney convinced Marcus to ride the wave of public interest generated by his sudden return and chart-topping single. Marcus reluctantly agreed, with one nonnegotiable condition—he refused to leave his family behind. Rodney accepted, though he admitted he was curious to see how well the "Allen" alias would hold up for Beth.

Rodney began booking appearances and boosting record sales. Whenever Marcus performed or appeared for interviews, Beth and Lizzie traveled with him. Katie joined them to help during the trips, taking on a nanny role so that "Beth Allen" could serve as Marcus's personal security.

Speculation arose in tabloids about his petite female security agent. Some questioned whether Marcus was truly safe, while others suggested he was simply loyal to his longtime team.

When asked about her, Marcus always replied, "I hired the best in the field when I hired Beth."

The media quickly dug into her background, learning she was a widowed veteran who had remarried and had a child. Once they confirmed she was legitimate, their curiosity faded.

After several months of traveling, Marcus told Rodney to pause all new appearances. The constant movement made him miss their peaceful island life, and he feared that repeated trips might lead someone to uncover their location.

A few months later, Marcus was notified that he had been nominated for several awards for his latest album. When asked if he would also present an award, he agreed—reluctantly.

His acceptance encouraged the organizers to invite him to perform again, but he declined. He didn't want the event to become centered around him, especially since he was already up for multiple categories. Disappointed but understanding, they thanked him for attending and confirmed he would present the award for Female Vocalist of the Year.

CHAPTER THIRTY SIX

The Donovan's fly back to Las Vegas with a dual purpose— the main being Lizzie's first birthday, and secondly, for the awards show.

Upon arriving at the mansion this time, the paparazzi are waiting for Marcus. They heard he was returning to present an award at the show and have been camped outside the mansion, waiting for weeks for his arrival.

Marcus and his team, always a step ahead, are prepared. Once they arrive at the airport, Mancuso gives them a heads-up about the media staked out at the mansion. Beth and Bobby easily escort Marcus and his parents into the mansion safely, with minimal distraction.

Mancuso then transports Katie and Lizzie in a separate SUV. Beth trusts Mancuso explicitly, but still gets nervous whenever she has to be apart from Lizzie.

The paparazzi have already dissipated by the time Katie and Lizzie arrive. Once the entire family is back together and settled in the mansion, Beth excuses herself, stating she wants to put Lizzie down for her nap. Worried, Marcus notices Beth looks tired.

"Babe are you OK?"

"I am just a bit tired my love. I might also try to take a quick nap. It has already been a busy day."

"Do you want me to join you?" he asks with a wink.

"No way my handsome husband, I actually want to get some rest."

She blows him a kiss from across the room and melts with love for this sweet man as she leaves.

Once inside their bedroom, Lizzie falls asleep peacefully, leaving Beth time to process her new situation. She had started feeling airsick mid-flight, immediately recognizing her symptoms.

Beth needs her special candy now, which only Katie can retrieve. She picks up her phone and sends a text for Katie to come to her room when available. Katie wastes no time proceeding to the main suite and, within minutes, knocks on the bedroom door. Beth answers, and Katie knows instantly by Beth's coloring that her suspicions are correct.

Without a word from Beth, Katie whispers,

"I know what will make you feel better my dear. Don't worry; Katie will take care of you honey."

Beth can't find the words to respond; she simply nods. Katie leaves the room, quietly closing the door behind her.

Within minutes, she returns to the master suite with ginger tea, promising she will arrange to go to the drugstore to retrieve Beth's favorite ginger candy. After drinking the tea, Beth snuggles into the overstuffed king-size bed and succumbs to slumber. About an hour later, the soft sounds of Lizzie cooing wake her.

Beth is relieved the tea, along with the short nap, appears to have temporarily subsided her nausea.

She picks up Lizzie, hugging her tightly.

"It looks like you will be a big sister my darling."

Beth changes the baby's clothing, then decides to change her own as well. After exiting the room, she heads to the kitchen to find Lizzie's milk and snack.

Upon entering, she finds Chef and Katie discussing meal prep. Beth notices the all-knowing look on both their faces. After noticing how it appears, Katie is the first to assure Beth of her loyalty.

"I promise Ms. Beth, I have not said anything about you." The chef stops Katie mid-sentence as she senses the tension building.

"Sorry ma'am, but I have been around for a while. Ginger tea is often a good remedy for alleviating nausea. I added in Katie's request for a somewhat bland dinner option—it was purely speculative on my part. I apologize to both of you for my assumptions. Please do not be upset with Katie because of me."

Beth flashes them both a sincere smile, trusting both women.

"I trust Katie tremendously; she always has my best interests in mind. I need to tell my husband before word gets out."

She places her finger to her lips in a hush gesture; both ladies nod, locking their lips and throwing away the key.

"So, what do we have for a snack for this precious angel of mine?"

The chef immediately responds, saying she will return with Miss Lizzie's bottle and snack.

As Beth takes a seat at the table, Katie rises to take Lizzie from her. Lizzie, always happy to see Katie, begins babbling, which makes them both smile at the happy baby.

When snack time is over, Katie adjourns to the playroom with Lizzie.

***

Beth makes her way through the mansion in search of Marcus. He has agreed to do a guest spot on a morning show tomorrow. She and Bobby will both be attending as his security detail. Even though they are all familiar with their standard protocols when attending events, she appreciates when the three of them gather and review beforehand.

***

After dinner, Beth and Marcus decide to call it an early night and retire, as he is committed to appear on an early morning show.

With Lizzie settled and already asleep, they talk as they usually do as they prepare for bed. During this nightly conversation, a wave of nausea hits Beth, and she instinctively places her hand on her flat stomach.

Momentarily confused, Marcus sees her go pale.

"Babe, are you…?"

He is about to ask if she is OK when he remembers he has seen this pale gray-green look on her face one other time. Afraid to say the words out loud, he raises his eyebrows in an unspoken question.

She responds with a shrug of her shoulders.

"Maybe, I mean, I think so."

Instinctively, she smiles as she raises her hand, crossing her fingers. They have not been trying for another baby, but truthfully, they have not tried to prevent it from happening either.

He crosses the room, taking her in his arms, he begins kissing her slowly.

"I never imagined I could love you anymore, but here we are, and my love for you is unimaginable now."

Their kiss deepens, and as it does every time since the very first, desire and passion take possession of their bodies. Later, they both claim it was their best lovemaking to date.

Truthfully, Beth smiles to herself; they claim this every time.

***

Not used to the sound of an early alarm, they reluctantly rise and begin preparing for Marcus's appearance on the morning show.

He prefers to do his own make-up and dress at the mansion rather than deal with the chaos of using the resources the studio makes available to him.

Beth is silently glad, as it allows her to hug and kiss her favorite superstar as he assumes the mega rock star persona. His outfits are all beautifully tailored to perfection, fitting his slim physique flawlessly. He is, after all, the hottest rock star, one who the world cannot get enough of.

For a split second, Beth wishes she could accompany him as his proud wife, openly admitting that he is her husband and the father of her child—or, due to recent circumstances, possibly her children.

As she stands staring at her phenomenal husband, preparing to be in a much sought-after interview, she doesn't hear him when he asks how she is feeling.

"Earth to Beth. Darling, are you OK?"

Hearing the concern in his voice, she gives him a thumbs-up just as they hear Katie knock on the door to retrieve Lizzie. She enters the suite, crossing the room to pick up Lizzie, since she will be her caretaker while they are away.

***

Once they are both fully dressed and prepared to leave, they proceed to the limo. Exiting the mansion, they find Bobby cheerfully greeting them with sarcasm.

"Good morning, Donovan family."

Marcus knows all too well that Bobby's joking attitude is because he knows Marcus is not a morning person.

"Good? How in the world did I get roped into an early morning show? I need to know. I might have to fire Rodney. I should be cuddling with my beautiful wife and enjoying breakfast with my baby."

He flashes his million-dollar smile at Bobby. Beth gives him a playful nudge as she states matter of fact,

"Time to go, Mr. Donovan. Beth Allen is at your service today."

Marcus beams at her with unmistakable pride and feigned insecurity as he asks,

"Beth, sit back here with me today, please."

Beth can't help but chuckle at his childlike request.

"Sorry sir, security detail rides shotgun.

She then closes the door behind him, opens the front passenger door, and seats herself.

Bobby is amused by their playful banter. He can't help but smile and shake his head in adoration at this perfect match.

***

When they arrive at the studio, Beth promptly exits the car to open the back passenger door of the limo for Marcus to exit.

In true star fashion, he steps out of the back seat with perfect posture and a smile to light up the world. As they stand together, waiting for Bobby to join them, she hears Marcus say softly to her,

"OK Beth, it is showtime."

CHAPTER THIRTY SEVEN

Marcus and his two security personnel proceed to the stage door, where they are met by a studio security team member. The young man allows them entrance when he instantly recognizes Marcus. Once inside, they are escorted to the green room to await their designated time slot.

Upon entering, they notice they are joining another celebrity already in the green room with his security agent. Marcus approaches him, greeting him as they introduce themselves and exchange pleasantries.

Beth and Bobby take their assigned stances and begin scanning the area.

Within minutes of their arrival, a production assistant arrives to retrieve the waiting man, leaving his security detail behind.

He is a young man who looks to be in his early thirties.

As Beth continues to observe the room, maintaining her professional status, she notices the young bodyguard watching her, following her every move. She gives him a nod but no smile, letting him know she is aware of his stares. He smiles anyway and continues to watch her as she remains in her ever-observant stance.

She is unfazed, as she has gotten used to the stares over the years. Most people do not believe a woman can be as proficient as a man in protecting an asset. She is always amused to see the expressions on their faces when they see her—a petite woman—protecting someone of Marcus Donovan's grandeur.

Marcus has now also noticed the young man's interest in his security team member and watches Beth intently. He has to agree—she is a sight to see. She stands stoic, looking like the top-notch professional she is, alert and not fazed by the man's stares.

His mind often drifts back to the first day he met her—the day he watched her ace her security detail exercise. He has never doubted Beth could and would protect him as well, if not better, than any man.

Marcus crosses the room to Bobby and whispers, trying to appear as if he was saying something of importance, but instead, he says,

"That young man seems to be taken with my wife. Little does he know she could kick his butt with one hand tied behind her back."

Bobby looks at his friend's faint smile, trying not to laugh, instead he nods in response.

Marcus is now walking away, heading toward Beth, when the production assistant notifies him he is on after the commercial break.

As Bobby and Beth move in to join Marcus, the assistant tells him that his security detail has to stay in the green room while he is on the air. In a tone of matter-of-fact, Marcus calmly states his manager prearranged for his security team to accompany him as far as the camera crew.

The PA nods and leads the way. After all, he is the buzz of the station this morning, and exceptions are made for celebrities of less status all the time. This is Marcus Donovan.

The interview goes off as promised. They comply, and no questions are asked about his frequent disappearing acts. However, they do throw in a few hints about it, stating that his downtime seemed successful as his new releases are going straight to the top of the charts.

Marcus, smiling, comments back,

"When you can remove yourself from the constant camera lens, it is amazing how the mind and soul open. If you listen to the quiet, the creative process becomes the forefront."

The subject then drops and shifts to his current award nominations. The ten-minute interview concludes as the morning show anchors thank Marcus for coming in. They tell him they would feel honored if he chose to return to perform one of his new songs soon.

He does not commit to it but jokingly says,

"Well, if we make it happen, can we do it in the last hour of your show? Normally, I like to sit and have coffee before venturing out."

He gives them his brilliant smile and a short laugh. Beth can see all the women on the set sigh with admiration. That smile is so damn sexy, and he is all hers.

Then, just like that, Marcus and his security detail exit the building, enter the waiting limo and go home.

***

Katie purchases a pregnancy test as promised, but Beth postpones taking it. She is unsure whether her reluctance is due to the fear of being too early or of it being negative.

Marcus begs Beth to take the test on the day of the awards ceremony. He is excited about adding another product of their love to the world. He understands Beth's concerns and assures her he will be happy regardless of the results.

"Babe if it's negative, it just means we need more practice."

"You are so silly honey. I love you so much."

Beth gives in to Marcus's reasoning, as she does most of the time where he is concerned. They both wait patiently in the master bathroom for the results to show.

When the timer on Marcus's phone goes off, they both take a deep breath before looking. Two blue lines indicate a positive outcome. Marcus yells with joy as he embraces Beth, swinging her in circles.

"I love you so much!" he gushes.

"I love you more. We are going to have another baby."

When they are back in the bedroom, he takes possession of her mouth, and as if her body has a mind of its own, their desire to become one takes over. In the aftermath of their lovemaking, she feels Marcus place his hand on her flat stomach. She can feel the emotion in his touch.

She turns, searching his eyes; seeing the raw emotion in them, she chokes back tears. Placing light kisses along his neck.

"How did we get so lucky to find each other and create an awesome family? I love you more every day."

He nods before lifting her face to his.

"No matter who I am—Marcus, Donnie, or whatever name you want to call me—I will always love you. I cannot wait for the day I celebrate you with the world."

Beth breaks free from his lips and giggles.

"We will have to wait on the latter for now; today, we're celebrating your hopeful wins tonight."

Breathless, Marcus mutters,

"I already won. You will always be my favorite award Beth."

"Good to know, Mr. Donovan," are the last legible words spoken between them as their passion takes over again.

They are two unlikely people who have found love and happiness in each other—all the while, the world around them remains oblivious.

***

Today, the entire team, Bobby, Mancuso, and Beth will all work the awards show with Marcus. Bobby will stay with the car, while Mancuso and Beth ensure Marcus gets securely inside the venue. Once inside, security is provided by a private company specializing in event security, including award shows.

Fans pack the streets to witness all the celebrities' arrivals. Due to the extreme size of the crowd, they are positive Marcus's fans are here in abundance.

Bobby brings the car to a halt in front of the red carpet.

"Showtime. Team, I have got the right side today. Marcus, are you ready?"

"I am, but you know I must greet my fans for a minute, right?"

"We wouldn't expect anything else boss man. I'll keep the limo here for a few extra minutes, so do your greeting quick."

They exit the car. Marcus waves, thanking his fans for their love and support before Beth and Mancuso whisk him down the aisle of velvet ropes lining the red carpet. Bobby then slowly pulls away, with fans still screaming Marcus's name.

As Marcus walks on the red carpet, Beth and Mancuso take their stance on the sidelines, remaining observant. Marcus's parents, who have arrived separately, now join Marcus before entering the venue.

Staff escorts Marcus and his parents to their assigned seating near the front of the event. Meanwhile, Beth and Mancuso are directed to a general area backstage to view the event via a monitor with other security personnel.

Beth wishes she could sit beside Marcus, holding his hand, anticipating his wins. Mancuso notices her sadness, giving her a brief smile.

"Mrs. Allen, this is the job you signed up for. Only you can decide to do something else."

"I know, but we can't. Not yet."

"Let's take our seats then; it will be a long day."

He is right. It is a long day, but Marcus shines, winning several awards. Each time he speaks, his acceptance speech of gratitude has embedded meanings—ones she recognizes as being for her and their children.

When she thinks she cannot love him anymore, he proves her wrong once again.

CHAPTER THIRTY EIGHT

Awakened by Marcus and Lizzie's soft whispers Beth smiles. She loves these intimate moments shared by just the three of them.

"Good morning Mr. Award-Winning Music Man."

"I'm sorry babe. We didn't mean to wake you. I was about to take Lizzie to breakfast. You need your rest—sleep a little longer."

She senses the love and concern in his words.

"How did I get so lucky to find you? Such a loving man in my life."

"Well darling, if you remember correctly, you applied for the position, and I hired you."

This was an ongoing banter between them.

"Mancuso tricked me into that interview."

However, the glimmer in her eyes told him a different story.

"Best hire to date," he teased.

She tossed one of the pillows in his direction.

"Lizzie, Mommy wants a pillow fight first thing this morning!"

He releases the toddler.

"Let's get Mommy!"

Lizzie trots toward the bed, trying to reach it before her daddy. Beth scoops up her daughter and begins smothering her with tiny kisses as Lizzie giggles.

Marcus, who had slid onto the bed from the foot, joins his favorite girls and places a light kiss on his wife's lips.

"Good morning my love."

"Morning Mr. Donovan. Love you more."

"Impossible."

"Prove it."

"I'm more than happy to oblige."

He takes her in his arms, and the kiss is not innocent this time. The not-so-subtle intent is clear, and they both know where it will lead. Beth is the first to pull away.

"Whew, that heated up fast."

"It always does, darling—it always does."

She still blushes when she thinks of the desire only he can ignite inside her. Taking a deep breath, she catches the twinkle in his eye as he watches her regain her composure.

He knows, without a shadow of a doubt, that he will never tire of this remarkable woman he's been blessed with.

She smiles at him, and he knows exactly what she is thinking: *to be continued.*

"Marcus my love, I am so proud of you. Your awards are more than well-deserved, and your indirect reference to Lizzie and me did not go unnoticed."

"Thanks babe. The only thing that would've made my night perfect was if you were by my side."

She felt the heartfelt sincerity in his statement and knew it was true. She felt the same way. These were the moments when she briefly felt ready to live their life publicly. However, they both knew the timing wasn't right. They desired privacy—not just for him anymore, but for Lizzie and their unborn child.

Still, they could live openly as *Mr. and Mrs. Donnie Allen* in Oklahoma, with the ranch house now completed months ago. Chloe had been assisting with the furnishings and staying in constant contact.

Marcus is surprised when he hears her next, unsuspected statement.

"I think it's time to move to the ranch house when we leave Las Vegas in a few days."

"You want to go to Oklahoma now—and not return to the island?"

She was confused by his question. She knew he preferred the seclusion of the island, but the plan was always to spend time on the ranch as well.

"Yes. Don't you want to go to the ranch?"

"Of course. I'm ready for ranch life. I know you've been working closely with Chloe; I just wasn't aware it was already complete."

"Whatever's not finished, we can complete together—make it ours. Besides, I'm thrilled at the thought of having a real nursery, one we can design together."

"I know babe. I'm sorry you didn't have a proper nursery before Lizzie's birth."

"Marcus, I don't regret any of our decisions—past or present."

"Truthfully, I'm ready to live our lives as Donnie and Beth, I have been for a while."

"I want to go out in public with my husband. I'm proud to be your wife. A wife likes to show off her husband, and I can't wait to show off mine to the entire community."

"Well, you know, we can share our secret with the world anytime—just say the word."

"You know how much I love you, and how proud I am of you. But we have our children to protect. Fame almost broke you. Imagine what it could do to your children."

"I know—and I agree. I want you to know that whenever you're ready to walk into my world as my wife, I'll be the proudest man on the planet. I was ready to share my love for you three years ago. You changed my world. Husbands like to show off their wives too."

He places another light kiss on her lips, then scoops Lizzie into his arms and heads toward the door.

"I guess you'd better call Chloe and tell her the Allens are on their way home. I'll talk to Bobby while I feed this little munchkin."

He nuzzles Lizzie's neck, and she giggles.

"Let's go find waffles, my little angel."

"Bye-bye, Mommy."

Beth feels an excited tingle run down her spine as the door closes behind them. The freedom of a small community will allow them to live openly. She'll get to design and decorate her baby's nursery. Her mind races with everything she wants to do once they're at the ranch.

She laughs softly to herself.

"Whoa, slow down a minute sista. This is not a race—Rome wasn't built in a day."

She crosses the bedroom and enters the massive bathroom, deciding to call Chloe after her shower and breakfast with her family.

Her sudden movement instantly reminds her of why they call it *morning sickness.* Smiling, she rubs her still-flat stomach.

"Looks like you're going to be an Okie, little one."

Thankfully, she's stashed her ginger candy everywhere. She locates her remedy, pops one in her mouth, disrobes, and steps into the shower.

Showered and dressed, she exits the master suite to meet her family in the kitchen. Right now, her main priority is coffee and dry toast. Entering, she finds Bobby and Marcus enjoying waffles with Lizzie. The toddler, covered in syrup, smiles as her mother enters.

"Oh my! I see who's next for a morning bath."

Bobby rises, making his way towards the sticky toddler.

"Bob-Bob at your service my lady. Let's get you all washed up and ready to go home to see Aunt Chloe."

Bobby can be heard gently humming *Home on the Range* as he exits the room with Lizzie.

Marcus rises from his chair and crosses the room to embrace Beth in his arms. She immediately relaxes, never realizing the anxious tension in her shoulders until his embrace melts it away.

"I guess everyone's excited about our new home. Are you sure you're ready for our next adventure in a new location?"

Beth looks up, meeting his eyes, and gently plants a light kiss on his lips.

"I'm ready to learn everything there is to learn about ranch life in Oklahoma. With you by my side as Donnie, we'll live our best life in plain sight."

"If I didn't love you and your plans so much, I might be nervous—but I'm not."

The next kiss, initiated by Marcus, is intense and heats up rapidly. Beth breaks away only long enough to whisper,

"Oklahoma, the Allens are coming home."

Not the end—*love never ends.*

Adventures of Marcus and Beth to be continued in the sequel: **Donovan: Living in Plain Sight**

DONOVAN:
Living in Plain Sight
Sneak Peek

The time has finally come. Living under the names Donnie and Beth Allen still felt surreal, as if they were walking into a dream, one they prayed would never turn into a nightmare.

For three years, they had beaten the odds—slipping quietly out of Marcus's life of chaos and into the refuge of Allure, a private haven known only to a select few.

Every day had been a gift. Each sunrise was without intrusion, each sunset without fear. Marcus and Beth had stitched together a world where both could experience peace and solitude raising their daughter, Lizzie.

Yet Beth knew the island was never meant to be permanent; it was only the first step. Oklahoma would be the actual test, hoping not to expose the secrets they tried so hard to keep hidden.

Now, standing on the edge of yet another turning point, she hoped their luck would hold. Another layer of their plan was ready to unfold, another step into the life they only dared to imagine.

It was time to test whether the world had room for Donnie and Beth Allen—or if the truth of their lives would come crashing through the walls of their carefully built sanctuary.

ACKNOWLEDGMENTS

How do I start to thank everyone who encouraged me during this unexpected journey, one I secretly began over a year ago. One Sunday morning I decided to put my imagination on paper, I only dreamed for where we are today.

Once I shared my secret to only those closest to me, their love and support encouraged me to complete my dream.

Dad- My ride or die. Without you, your dreams and guidance, none of my success would be possible. You asked to read the chapters faster than I could create them. With your positive feedback you gave me confidence. I love you dad, and your story is the next to be published.

Debbie & Jackie- There are no words to express how thankful I am to have you both in my life, always in my corner, forever, no matter what the situation. Besties forever.

Debbie, thanks for being a BETA reader, all your support and every input you have given me since, listening sincerely and patiently, as I talk out ideas. Love you.

Jackie, thanks for always being my biggest cheerleader. Blessed to have you and your support. I hope you enjoy the story as much as your husband did. You have assured me you will buy the first hardcopy; I'm holding you to it. Love you.

Gena- You agreed to be a BETA reader, even though romance novels are not your preferred genre. Your quirky notes, both fun and professional, were greatly appreciated. You even surprised yourself with how immersed you became in the story. Love you.

Pete- Thanks, I know you kinda got roped into becoming a BETA reader, knowing romance novels are not in your wheelhouse, since it doesn't include numbers. Your idea to name the island Allure was perfect. If this book becomes a trilogy, it will be because of you. Love you

Colbie- Your insight and honesty was very helpful. Thanks for agreeing to be a BETA reader.

Diana- Thanks for your support and being a BETA reader.

Tim (Timmy)- Thank you for providing me with much insight due to your previous experience in publishing. Your feedback was very helpful. You rounded out my mixed bag of BETA readers, Thanks.

Eddie, Jerome and Greg- How do I thank all of you for the assistance in getting my manuscript in the hands of those who needed it. I am blessed to have you all in my life and supporting this crazy dream I had, promising to buy your wives a copy. Love you.

Harry and team- My project manager. You have been patient with all my questions and corrections. Thank you for everything. Let's make this book a success, and the sequel that follows.

Thanks to my family, my biggest fans, Jeff, Andy, as well as: Gavin, Josie, River, Beverly.

To my family and friends, not named, Thank You. You were excited for me as I took the leap into this wonderful journey. My hope is to leave a legacy for my grandbabies, showing them you are never too old to dream.

Thank you to the readers who chose to take a chance on a first-time author. I hope you were immersed in the journeys of Marcus and Beth, and you will join me on their next adventure.

Most importantly, *Thank You to my Lord Jesus for paving every step of this journey for me, you get all the glory.*

Carolyn

www.ingramcontent.com/pod-product-compliance
Lightning Source LLC
Chambersburg PA
CBHW051258120626
46547CB00015B/1995